UNLOCKING TANNISHO

Shinran's Words on the Pure Land Path

UNLOCKING TANNISHO

Shinran's Words on the Pure Land Path

KENTETSU TAKAMORI

Translated and adapted by
Juliet Winters Carpenter

Ichimannendo Publishing, Inc.

Los Angeles   Tokyo

Unlocking Tannisho: Shinran's Words on the Pure Land Path
By Kentetsu Takamori
Published by Ichimannendo Publishing, Inc. (IPI)
970 West 190th Street, Suite 920, Torrance, California 90502
info@i-ipi.com   www.i-ipi.com
© 2011 by Kentetsu Takamori. All rights reserved.
Translated and adapted by Juliet Winters Carpenter.

NOTES TO THE READER:
In the process of producing the English translation, this book has been widely adapted by the author
in close collaboration with the translator.
Throughout this book ages are given according to the traditional way of reckoning in Japan (in which the
first year of life is counted as one rather than zero, and the age increases by one at each New Year's).

Jacket design by Kazumi Endo
Text format design by Kazuyo Nakamura (Michiyoshi Design Laboratory Inc.)
Japanese calligraphy by Taizan Kimura
Photographs by amanaimages and Tetsuji Yamamoto

First edition, April 2011
Printed in Japan
15 14 13 12 11   1 2 3 4 5 6 7 8 9 10

No part of this book may be reproduced in any form without permission from the publisher.

This book was originally published in Japanese by Ichimannendo Publishing under the title of *Tannisho wo hiraku*.
© 2008 by Kentetsu Takamori

P. 18: "Shinran taught that if you say the nembutsu out of sincere faith in Amida's salvation, . . ."
Kazuo Kasahara et al. In *Shosetsu nihonshi* [Detailed History of Japan; rev. ed.], Yamakawa Publishing, 1978.

P. 19: "When the inclination to say the nembutsu arises in you, . . ."
Kazuo Kasahara. "Tannisho: *mayoi oki jinsei e no oinaru shirube*" ["*Tannisho*: guidance for living"]
in *President* magazine, December 1984 issue.

Distributed in the United States and Canada by AtlasBooks Distribution, a division of BookMasters, Inc.
30 Amberwood Parkway, Ashland, Ohio 44805
1-800-BookLog   www.atlasbooks.com

Distributed in Japan by Ichimannendo Publishing
2-4-5F Kanda-Ogawamachi, Chiyoda-ku, Tokyo 101-0052
info@10000nen.com   www.10000nen.com

Library of Congress Control Number: 2011924319
ISBN 978-0-9790471-5-2

ISBN 978-4-925253-48-2

Contents

Introduction .... *ix*

Translator's Foreword .... *xii*

Part One
Tannisho: Amplified Translation *1*

Part Two
A Guide to *Tannisho*:
Close Translation and Clarification of Easily Misunderstood Passages *15*

Close Translations of *Tannisho*

    Section I *17*

    Section II *29*

    Section III *43*

    Section IV *49*

    Section V *55*

    Section VI *59*

    Section VII *63*

    Section VIII *67*

    Section IX *71*

    Section X *77*

    Epilogue *82*

1 How Easy It Is to Misunderstand *Tannisho* *18*
    —Clarification of Section I of *Tannisho* (1 of 4)—

2 Amida's Salvation Happens in This Life *20*
    —Clarification of Section I of *Tannisho* (2 of 4)—

3 "The Sole Requirement Is Faith" *23*
  —Clarification of Section I of *Tannisho* (3 of 4)—

4 "No Need for Good, No Fear of Evil": What Does This Really Mean? *26*
  —Clarification of Section I of *Tannisho* (4 of 4)—

5 Does Other-Power Mean That We Sit Back and Do Nothing? *30*
  —Clarification of Section II of *Tannisho* (1 of 4)—

6 "Only Say the Nembutsu": The Meaning of "Only" *34*
  —Clarification of Section II of *Tannisho* (2 of 4)—

7 The Real Meaning of Shinran's "I Do Not Know in the Least" *37*
  —Clarification of Section II of *Tannisho* (3 of 4)—

8 Because Amida's Vow Is True *40*
  —Clarification of Section II of *Tannisho* (4 of 4)—

9 "If Even a Good Person Will Attain Salvation,
  All the More So Will an Evil Person" *44*
  —Clarification of Section III of *Tannisho*—

10 The Real Meaning of "Quickly Attaining Buddhahood" *50*
  —Clarification of Section IV of *Tannisho*—

11 Funerals and Memorial Services Are Not for the Dead *56*
  —Clarification of Section V of *Tannisho*—

12 No Disciples: Shinran's Love for One and All *60*
  —Clarification of Section VI of *Tannisho*—

13 What Happens When We Are Saved by Amida? *64*
  —Clarification of Section VII of *Tannisho*—

14 The Great Faith and the Great Practice *68*
    —Clarification of Section VIII of *Tannisho*—

15 "No Desire to Dance in Joy": Shinran's Lack of Joy
    Is Only Half the Story *72*
    —Clarification of Section IX of *Tannisho*—

16 What Is "Namu Amida Butsu"? *78*
    —Clarification of Section X of *Tannisho*—

17 The Reality of Self-Power and the Ocean of Other-Power Faith *84*
    —Clarification of the Epilogue of *Tannisho* (1 of 2)—

18 The Universal Purpose of Life *87*
    —Clarification of the Epilogue of *Tannisho* (2 of 2)—

Glossary *91*

Bibliography *96*

Map of Places That Appear in the Text *97*

Timeline of the Development of Pure Land Buddhism *98*

Appendix
Japanese Text of *Tannisho* *001*
    (The Appendix reads from right to left and in reverse page order, from page 001 through page 024.)

Introduction

In spring of 1944, at the age of sixteen, I volunteered to join the Japanese Imperial Naval Air Service and was trained as a fighter pilot. Months before the end of the Pacific War, still a teenager, I watched as one after another of my comrades took off in an airplane loaded with explosives and just enough fuel for a one-way trip. Their orders were to crash their planes into allied warships and aircraft carriers in a desperate, last-ditch attempt to win an unwinnable war.

The treatment meted out to kamikaze pilots in training was cruel and brutal. We were constantly beaten, trained only to obey and die. We were brainwashed, told that to give up our lives was a great honor and that through our sacrifice we would not only save our sacred nation and serve the emperor but be granted immortality. Still too young to make the list, I knew it was only a matter of time before my turn came—yet deep down I prayed to live, as did my comrades. All of the doomed pilots tried to find meaning in that desperate situation. I well remember that as their only companion on that final flight, many chose to take along the book *Tannisho* and the message of Shinran.

After the war, my life fortunately spared, I turned my attention to that small book and its great teachings. My encounter with them transformed my life and filled me with renewed purpose. I still grow hot with anger when I think of how my friends and I were deceived, instilled with the idea that throwing away our lives was somehow beautiful. Yet I am grateful beyond words to have been granted the happiness of knowing the truth. I have dedicated my life to deepening my understanding of, and sharing with others, the same undying principles that were a ray of bright hope to those youths setting off on their dark and hopeless journeys.

Sixty-five years have gone by since Japan's defeat. With the collapse of the old Imperial Japan and the advent of a new era, the nation went through a time of wholesale physical and spiritual reconstruction. New values replaced the old ones. The emperor was not a god at all, it turned out, but a mere human being. Japanese people were not divine or special, either, but brothers and sisters of the whole human race with freedom to choose for themselves how to live and, more importantly, find out why to live. Instead of resigning themselves to bleak fate, they could sow the seeds of future happiness. With these ideas as a mainstay—ideas rooted in the teachings of Shinran—Japan rose from the rubble and found courage to go on.

Shinran's ideas are truly liberating. He pointed out that to attain enduring happiness is the purpose of life, and that such happiness can be attained while we are yet alive. He preached the absolute equality of all people and the infinite preciousness of a single human life. This truth became the mainstay of the Japanese spirit in the postwar era, underlying contemporary Japanese political, economic, and educational systems, as well as other cultural fields. This connection helps to explain Shinran's steady rise in prominence since the war. Even though he lived over seven hundred and fifty years ago, in 1995 a popular television show dedicated an entire program to Shinran as the historical figure who was studied, discussed, and admired more than any other during the twentieth century in Japan.

Interest in *Tannisho* continues to grow. Many postwar writers, thinkers, and newsmakers have focused on studying its philosophy, and until very recently as many as ten commentaries were published each year. The sheer number of commentaries on this amazing book tells us both how beloved it is and how mysterious.

What is the source of *Tannisho*'s mesmerizing appeal? Why do the words of Shinran go on captivating readers' minds and hearts? Let me briefly explain the background of this treasure from the late thirteenth century.

"Even a good person can be born in the Pure Land; how much more so an evil person!" These unforgettable words are from Section III of *Tannisho*. The book is filled with similarly haunting statements and challenging concepts. Yuien (1222–89), one of Shinran's leading disciples, is believed to be the author. The title, which means "Lamenting the Deviations," refers to Yuien's sorrow about common misrepresentations of Shinran's core teachings and his determination to set the record straight.

Chronologically, *Tannisho* falls squarely between two other widely read gems of medieval Buddhist literature: *An Account of My Hut*, a contemplative essay on the transiency of life written in 1212 by reclusive monk Kamo no Chomei (ca. 1155–1216), and *Essays in Idleness*, a collection of musings on a variety of topics by priest and scholar Kenko (d. 1352?). Of the three, *Tannisho* is particularly renowned for a literary style of such beauty and economy that many people have been inspired to commit the entire work to memory.

Strange as it may seem, despite its iconic status *Tannisho* has been widely known for less than a century. Five hundred years ago, the book was put under seal after the priest Rennyo forbade readers from showing it indiscriminately to the uninitiated. Then even Shinran scholars and followers grew wary of the book, and very few people knew of its existence until it happened to come under renewed scrutiny in the late nineteenth century. Today *Tannisho* is inseparably connected with the teachings of Shinran and is considered an apt introduction to his thought. It continues to provide spiritual comfort and strength for countless readers, just as it did for my comrades long ago.

Just as Rennyo foretold, however, *Tannisho* has proved a two-edged sword. For example, the passage quoted above, with its assertion that salvation belongs "all the more so [to] an evil person," inspired some to proclaim early on that since Amida loves evildoers, the more evil we do, the better! Shinran's teachings thus came under fire for "creating evildoers." Even today, Shinran scholars, not to mention ordinary readers, are prone to make fundamental errors of interpretation. As Rennyo well knew, the core truths of *Tannisho* often prove elusive to those without proper guidance.

The peril of approaching *Tannisho* unaided is real. Intended originally as a hidden treasure for the inner few, in the hands of the wrong reader the book is like a razor, capable of inflicting grievous harm. The only way to prevent an outcome of bitter regret for oneself and others is to read *Tannisho* armed with a full understanding of Shinran's thought.

Tannisho commentaries abound. Regrettably, they tend to offer freewheeling interpretations that emphasize the authors' personal experiences and beliefs. In *Unlocking Tannisho*, I have drawn on Shinran's magnum opus, *Teaching, Practice, Faith, Enlightenment*—which he continued to rewrite and polish throughout his life—as well as many other of his works in an effort to see *Tannisho* in its original light and so clarify its true meaning. I believe that relying on Shinran's own words is the best way—the only way—to get to the bottom of this crucially important text.

Now through this English-language version of my translation and commentary, *Tannisho* embarks on yet another journey. I am grateful to Juliet Carpenter and many others for their unstinting labors in helping to bring Shinran's words to readers around the world. The opportunity to engage in dialogue about *Tannisho* with readers is something I look forward to very much. Everyone's comments and criticisms are sincerely welcome.

Kentetsu Takamori
Spring 2011

Translator's Foreword

Tannisho ("Lamenting the Deviations"), a beloved thirteenth-century text of seminal importance in True Pure Land Buddhism, is far from easy to understand. To disseminate its profound message, Kentetsu Takamori undertook to render the original into clear, modern language and also to discuss and resolve common misunderstandings that have long clouded its interpretation. To assist with each of these goals, the English version of his book follows a rather unusual format, as explained below.

Part One contains my translation of Takamori's groundbreaking, amplified rendition into modern Japanese of *Tannisho* (all except sections XI–XVIII, which are presented in digest form). Takamori has clarified the true meaning of the classic in readily accessible language for our time. Notes alongside the text and a glossary at the back of the book are added for the convenience of readers unfamiliar with Buddhist concepts, terms, and personages.

Part Two contains in-depth explanations of certain significant passages which, though widely admired and often quoted, are frequently misunderstood. While the mysterious and beautiful language of *Tannisho* has always drawn many readers and generated interest in Shinran, this uncommonly rich and difficult text is fraught with dangers of misinterpretation. Here Takamori returns to the source—Shinran's own words—in order to illuminate the true meaning of some of the most important and most generally misinterpreted passages of *Tannisho*.

Scattered throughout Part Two is a second English translation of *Tannisho*, one that aims to preserve the ambiguities and resonance of the original text. The clarifications necessarily refer to this close translation, as Takamori cites the original frequently to show how errors have crept into popular understanding of Shinran's thought. After reading Part Two, readers are urged to return to Part One to reacquaint themselves with Takamori's rendition that resolves ambiguities while maintaining the grace and integrity of the original.

Perhaps a word is in order on the overall construction of *Tannisho*. Of the work's eighteen sections, the first ten are direct transmissions of the words of Shinran as remembered and recorded by the writer, believed to be a disciple of Shinran's named Yuien. In the remaining eight, the writer takes Shinran's teachings as a measure for the correction of heretical ideas that had gained currency at the time. There are two prefaces, one for the entire work and another for the latter half, as well as an epilogue with an account of Shinran's banishment. Some one hundred and fifty years after the work was first written, Shinran's descendant Rennyo (1415–99) appended a final brief warning against showing the book indiscriminately to those with little grounding in Buddhism.

No longer hidden, *Tannisho* is a work of singular beauty as well as deep spiritual challenges and insights, a work to be read and pondered and cherished. It is my hope, and the hope of all who have aided in the creation of this English-language book, that many new readers will indeed use it to "unlock" *Tannisho*.

Finally, I would like to take this opportunity to thank all those who worked with me so patiently and encouraged me, spending uncountable hours in deep discussion and debate. Time and again, as he did previously with *You Were Born for a Reason* (Ichimannendo Publishing, Los Angeles, 2006), Takamori went over my work carefully, reading and painstakingly revising back-translations. After discussion, I would incorporate his changes into the English, which would again be back-translated for his approval. The endless back-and-forth was often exhausting, but Takamori's dedication and enthusiasm fueled everyone's energy and spirit. I would also like to thank Dr. Alfred Bloom and the other readers from around the world who took time to look over an early version of the book and offer helpful comments and corrections. Needless to say, any infelicities or problematic phrasings that remain are my fault alone. Lastly, I must thank Bruce Carpenter, my husband, for his unfailing encouragement and support.

Juliet Winters Carpenter
Spring 2011

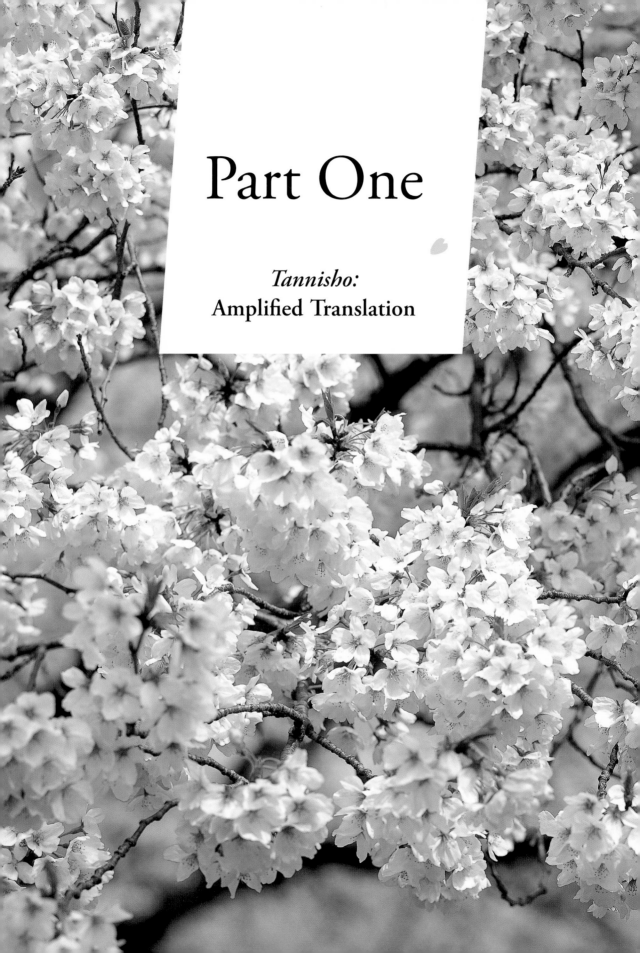

Part One

Tannisho:
Amplified Translation

Preface

As I privately cast my foolish mind over the time when Master Shinran was alive and compare it with the present day, I cannot help lamenting that there are deviations from what the master taught us directly about true faith. I am concerned that doubts and confusion will arise in the study and transmission of his teaching. How is it possible, without being fortunate enough to encounter a good teacher, to obtain salvation through other-power faith?[1] Private opinion must not be allowed to distort the true meaning of other-power.

With this in mind I have noted down a few of Master Shinran's unforgettable sayings, which still echo in my ears. My sole wish is to dispel the doubts of fellow Shinran followers.[2]

I

When, being saved by the inconceivable power of Amida Buddha's[3] Vow,[4] your birth in Amida's Pure Land[5] is assured beyond any doubt and the desire to say the nembutsu[6] erupts within you, in that instant you are clasped fast by Amida, never to be abandoned, thus entering into absolute happiness. Amida's salvation makes no distinction whatever between young and old or good and evil. Know that faith alone is essential—faith in the truth of the Vow with no possibility of doubt.

How is it possible that even an evil person can be saved merely through faith in the Vow? This is the true value of Amida's Primal Vow: it was established precisely to save the monstrous sinner whose blind passions[7] rage and whose sins weigh heavy. It follows that anyone saved by Amida's Vow has no need to do good deeds for the sake of their salvation, because no greater good exists than the nembutsu bestowed on us by Amida. Also, whatever evil such a person may commit, he is free from concern or fear, because no evil can hinder salvation by Amida's Vow.

This is what the master said.

[1] The faith bestowed by Amida Buddha.

[2] Those who learn, believe, and convey the teachings of Shinran.

[3] Amida Buddha: The master of all buddhas.

[4] Amida's pledge to save all sentient beings into absolute happiness without fail.

[5] Amida's Pure Land: The world of bliss inhabited by Amida Buddha.

[6] Nembutsu: The recitation of Amida Buddha's Name, "Namu Amida Butsu."

[7] Blind passions: Lust, anger, jealousy, and other delusions of the heart that trouble and torment us.

II

You have come to see me all the way from Kanto,[8] crossing over mountains and rivers of more than ten provinces without regard for your lives, intending solely to verify the path to birth in the land of utmost bliss.[9] But if you suspect me of withholding knowledge of some path to birth other than the nembutsu of Amida's Vow,[10] or knowledge of some secret text, you are greatly mistaken.

If you have so little faith in me, then go to Nara[11] or Mount Hiei.[12] There are many fine scholars there, so go ask them all about the essence of birth in the Pure Land.

As for me, I simply trust in the teaching of Honen:[13] "Believe in the Vow, say the nembutsu, and be saved by Amida Buddha." There is nothing else.

Some people claim that saying the nembutsu is an act that causes people to fall into hell;[14] but whether the nembutsu is in fact the seed that will cause me to be born in the Pure Land or an act for which I will fall into hell, I have no idea. Even if I find I have been deceived by Master Honen and end up falling into hell because of the nembutsu, I will have no regrets.

For if I could attain buddhahood by carrying out any other practice besides the nembutsu, and then fell into hell for saying it, I would feel regret. But as I am incapable of doing any good at all, I have no other possible destination but hell.

Given that Amida's Primal Vow is true, then the teachings of Śākyamuni,[15] which concern only the Vow, cannot be false. If the sermons of Śākyamuni are true, then the commentaries of Shan-tao,[16] who explained them faithfully, cannot contain lies. If the commentaries of Shan-tao are true, then how can there be any falsehood in the sayings of Master Honen, who conveyed them faithfully? If the sayings of Honen are true, then how can what I say be empty, since I have faithfully conveyed what he said?

This, in short, is my faith. Beyond this, whether to believe in the nembutsu or discard it is entirely up to each of you to decide.

This is what the master said.

[8] A broad region consisting today of Tokyo and six other prefectures.

[9] The land of utmost bliss: The Pure Land.

[10] The nembutsu of Amida's Vow: The nembutsu said without a remnant of doubt in Amida's Vow.

[11] The old capital of Japan, south of Kyoto; site of the influential temple Kofukuji.

[12] Mountain on the border between Kyoto and Shiga prefectures; site of the head temple of the Tendai sect of Buddhism.

[13] The founder of Pure Land Buddhism in Japan (1133–1212), and Shinran's teacher.

[14] A realm of suffering in the next life brought on by one's evil deeds.

[15] The historical Buddha (ca. 560–480 BC).

[16] One of the most important figures in Pure Land Buddhism in China (613–81).

III

Even a good person can be born in the Pure Land; how much more so an evil person!

Although this is the truth, people commonly say, "Even an evil person can be born in the Pure Land, so naturally a good person can." This way of thinking seems reasonable at first, but it goes against Amida's intention in making the Vow. Amida Buddha saw that human beings are each a mass of blind passions, desperately evil without a hope of salvation, and so he promised, "Entrust yourselves to me; I will save you without fail." Yet "good people" think in their vanity that they can resolve the question of their eternal fate[17] through the good that they do, doubting the Primal Vow that Amida made after he discerned how completely evil humans are. Such people have no intention of entrusting themselves entirely to Amida. Therefore they are not in accord with Amida's Vow; they are not objects of the Vow.

But even such people, once they have become astonished at their true nature as perceived by Amida Buddha and left the question of their eternal fate in his hands, are assured of birth in the Pure Land after death.

It is impossible for us, filled with blind passions as we are, to free ourselves from the suffering of birth and death[18] through any practice whatever. Amida took pity on our condition and made his Primal Vow with the purpose of ensuring that evil people will attain buddhahood. Therefore it is precisely evil people, those who recognize that they have no hope of salvation and so entrust themselves to other-power,[19] who are the real focus of Amida's Vow.

This is why the master said that since even a virtuous person can be born in the Pure Land, so without question can one who is evil.

This is what the master said.

IV

Concerning compassion, there is a difference between the Buddhism of sages[20] and Pure Land Buddhism.[21]

Compassion in the Buddhism of sages means to take pity on other people and on all beings, cherish them, and nurture them.

[17] The question of their eternal fate: Whether they will sink into an eternity of suffering or gain everlasting happiness.

[18] The suffering of birth and death: Being born and dying repeatedly in a cycle of suffering and sorrow.

[19] The power of Amida Buddha.

[20] The Buddhism of sages: Tendai, Shingon, Zen, and other Buddhist sects whose devotees undertake ascetic discipline as a means to enlightenment.

[21] Buddhism which teaches salvation by Amida Buddha.

Yet however hard we may try, it is all but impossible to benefit others as we would like to do.

Compassion as taught in Pure Land Buddhism means quickly being saved through Amida's Primal Vow and becoming a person of the nembutsu,[22] attaining the enlightenment of a buddha[23] in the Pure Land and, with a mind of great compassion, freely benefiting others as one wishes.

In this life, however much we may feel sorry for others and want to do something for them in pity, ultimately we cannot save them. The compassion of the Buddhism of sages is inevitably limited. Therefore, the only way to attain the thoroughgoing mind of great compassion is to be saved through Amida's Primal Vow and become a person of the nembutsu.

This is what the master said.

V

I, Shinran, have never said the nembutsu even once for the repose of my departed mother and father. For when I remember my parents, it comes home to me that all living beings have, over the course of endless cycles of birth and death, at some point been father or mother, brother or sister to me. So in the next life I must become a buddha and help one and all, without discriminating.

Were the nembutsu a good act that we carried out on our own, we might direct the resulting merit toward our parents and so save them, but it is not and we cannot. Yet if we just quickly abandon self-power,[24] which seeks to fathom the Primal Vow, and obtain the enlightenment of a buddha in the Pure Land, then we can employ the power of a buddha[25] to help others, beginning with those who share close ties with us, whoever they may be and whatever world of suffering they may be in.

This is what the master said.

VI

Among those who believe only in Amida and say the nembutsu, there appear to be disputes about "my disciples" and "other people's disciples." This is an outrage.

I, Shinran, do not have even one disciple.

The reason is simple: if I could use my own devices to bring people to listen to Buddhism and say the nembutsu, I might well

[22] Person of the nembutsu: One who says the nembutsu on having received salvation from Amida Buddha.

[23] The enlightenment of a buddha: The highest of the fifty-two levels of enlightenment.

[24] Doubts and deliberations about Amida Buddha's Vow. See also Glossary, "mind of self-power."

[25] The power of a buddha: A buddha's power to guide suffering people to true happiness.

call them my disciples. But as attending to Buddhism and saying the nembutsu occur solely through the power of Amida, for me to claim any personal disciples would be the height of arrogance.

When conditions bring us together, we will be together, and when they lead us apart, we must part. Meeting and parting happen according to an intricate web of causes and conditions. No one should ever say that if you turn your back on your teacher and say the nembutsu under someone else, you cannot go to the Pure Land. Are people who say such things deluded into thinking that the faith bestowed by Amida comes from them, and that they can withdraw it if they wish? This is a deplorable error. Such an absurd claim must never be made.

When we encounter the true salvation of Amida, the depth of our debt to him becomes self-evident, and likewise our debt to our teachers.

This is what the master said.

VII

Anyone who is saved by Amida and says the nembutsu is blessedly free from all hindrances. Why? Because before one who has been saved by Amida, the gods of heaven and earth bow their heads in reverence, and demons and heretics can no longer offer any obstruction. No sin such a person may commit, however great, will cause him or her to suffer, nor can the results of the greatest good such a person may do possibly equal the joy of salvation; thus any such person enjoys absolute freedom and happiness.

This is what the master said.

VIII

The nembutsu is, for those saved by Amida, not a practice or a good deed. Since it is not uttered at one's own discretion, it cannot be called a practice. Since it is not uttered according to one's own judgment, it cannot be called an act of goodness. Since the nembutsu derives completely from the power of Amida and has nothing to do with the designs of the self, for those saying it who are already saved by Amida, it is not a practice or a good deed.

This is what the master said.

IX

"Although I say the nembutsu, I feel no leaping, dancing joy. Also, I have no wish to hurry to the Pure Land. Why is this?"

I asked the master these things frankly, and he replied, "The very same thought has struck me. Yuien, you feel the same way?"

The master continued, "When I think carefully about it, the wonder that I—someone without a hope of salvation—am saved ought to fill me with such boundless joy that I could dance forever, but my very lack of joy shows plainly that my birth in the Pure Land[26] is assured.

"It is blind passions that keep us from rejoicing when we naturally should. Amida perceived long ago that human beings are nothing but blind passions. When we are made to realize that the Primal Vow is for us, whose hearts are numb, we see all the more how precious it is.

"Further, having no thought of hurrying to the Pure Land, when we become even slightly ill we wonder forlornly if we will die. This is also the doing of the blind passions. These worlds[27] where since time without beginning[28] we have died and been born, again and again, are places of suffering and pain; and yet we think of this as our old home and find it hard to leave. That we have no longing whatever for the Pure Land of Amida, where we are sure to be born, shows the power and intensity of our blind passions.

"And yet, however reluctant we may be to leave, when our bonds to this world end and our strength to live fails, we will go to Amida's Pure Land. Amida takes special pity on those who have no thought of hurrying there. The more we are made to see our wretched state, the more reassuring Amida's great Vow becomes, and we realize that our birth in the Pure Land is assured. If I were filled with bubbling joy and wished to hurry off to the Pure Land, I might worry that as I had no blind passions, the Vow did not apply to me."

This is what the master said.

X

The true meaning of the nembutsu lies in the absence of human deliberation, for the wondrous nembutsu of other-power,[29] where the deliberations of self-power have been annihilated, is beyond

[26] Birth in the Pure Land: Being born in Amida's Pure Land as a buddha. See also Glossary, "birth."

[27] The realms of delusion and suffering. See also Glossary, "six realms of suffering."

[28] The eternity before one is born into the present life.

[29] The nembutsu of other-power: The nembutsu spoken through the power of Amida Buddha.

speech, beyond explanation, beyond imagination. It beggars human understanding.

This is what the master said.

Preface to the Latter Half of the Book

Back when Master Shinran was alive, those who wanted to gain the same faith as him and be born in Amida's Pure Land traveled all the way from Kanto to Kyoto to receive teachings directly from his lips, and so no great problems arose. However, I have heard that lately, with the increasing number of people who receive teaching from Shinran's disciples and say the nembutsu, heretical views that the master never taught have come to hold great sway. This is lamentable. Below I will set forth those heresies and errors.

XI

[Summary][30]
Although the "wondrous working of the Vow" and the "wondrous working of the Name" refer alike to the power of Amida's Vow, some people sowed confusion by making an issue of whether people said the nembutsu believing in one or the other. This section laments and refutes that heresy.

[30] As the heresies addressed in sections XI–XVIII are rarely encountered today, they are presented here in digest form.

XII

[Summary]
This section laments and refutes the erroneous assertion that people who do not study important Buddhist scriptures and commentaries cannot be born in Amida's Pure Land.

XIII

[Summary]
This section laments and refutes the erroneous assertion that people who are unafraid of evil—since Amida's Primal Vow saves us regardless of what evil we may commit—are actually taking pride in the Vow and therefore cannot attain birth in the Pure Land.

XIV

[Summary]
This section laments and refutes the erroneous assertion that since saying the nembutsu a single time will wipe out eight billion kalpas[31] of evil, we must devote ourselves to saying it as many times as possible.

[31] One kalpa is 432,000,000 years; the word is used to refer to an inconceivably long period of time.

XV

[Summary]
This section laments and refutes the erroneous assertion that once we have obtained faith, we can achieve enlightenment in this life, filled with blind passions as we are.

XVI

[Summary]
This section laments and refutes the erroneous assertion that those who have been saved by Amida must repent and experience a change of heart every time they become angry, commit a misdeed, quarrel with a fellow practitioner, or the like.

XVII

[Summary]
This section laments and refutes the erroneous assertion that anyone who is born on the outer edges of the Pure Land will eventually fall into hell.

XVIII

[Summary]
This section laments and refutes the erroneous assertion that after death, when we achieve the enlightenment of a buddha, the actual size of the buddha we become depends on the amount of our donations to Buddhism.

Epilogue

The above heresies all arose apparently because their proponents' faith diverged from that of Master Shinran. He once told me the following story. Master Honen had many disciples, but it seems that few of them had the same faith as him. Perhaps for this reason, a debate once took place between Shinran and some of his friends. A remark of Shinran's set it off.

"My faith is the same as Master Honen's," he said.

Several of the disciples, including Seikanbo and Nembutsubo,[32] heard this and went into a rage, denouncing it as an affront. They demanded angrily, "How can you, a lowly disciple, say that your faith is the same as that of our master, who is foremost in wisdom?"

Shinran replied, "Had I claimed to possess wisdom as great as Master Honen's or learning as vast, your anger would be justified; but in terms of faith that leads to birth in the Pure Land, there is no difference whatever. Our faith is one and the same."

Unable to accept this response, the others continued to challenge Shinran, demanding to know how he could say such a thing. In the end they were obliged to appeal to Honen for a ruling.

When he had heard the details, Honen said, "My faith is the faith that is granted by Amida, and so is Shinran's. They are exactly the same. Anyone whose faith is different from this cannot go to the Pure Land where I am going."

From this story it may be gathered that even back then, among those who believed solely in Amida and said the nembutsu were some whose faith differed from Shinran's. I am making the same point over and over, but I have set it all down here in writing.

As long as life clings to my frame like a dewdrop on a blade of dry grass, I will go on listening to the doubts of those who have accompanied me thus far and tell them what Master Shinran said. But it weighs on me that after I have left this world, heresies of all kinds will run rampant. That is why I have written down the master's words. When you find yourself confused by the contentions of people who spread false teachings such as those laid out here, carefully examine the sacred writings that reflect the late master's teachings and that he himself referred to.

Generally the scriptures consist of the truth, set forth exactly as it is, and the provisional or expedient—that which leads us to the truth. It was Master Shinran's fundamental intention that in reading the scriptures we should abandon the expedient and take up the real, leave the provisional and enter into the true. Let no one ever interpret sacred writings to suit himself. Be at utmost pains not to misconstrue their true meaning. I have excerpted a few important passages and included them in this book as a guide.

The master would often say this:

> Through untold aeons of deep deliberation, Amida worked out the Primal Vow. Its meaning is brought home to me through reflection, and I see that it was all for my sake alone. How thankful I am for the Primal Vow, which Amida bestirred himself to make for my salvation, burdened as I am with evil and sin beyond reckoning!

As I recall these heartfelt words of Shinran's, I find them not at all different from this wise saying of Shan-tao's:

> I know myself to be one who continues even now to commit great evil, one who is suffering and lost. For countless aeons I have been continually submerged in the sea of suffering, continually repeating birth and death, with never a chance in all eternity to leave this labyrinth.

I am humbly grateful for these words of Master Shinran where he uses himself as an example, no doubt to awaken us from the depths of delusion in which we slumber, dead to the depths of our own evil and the greatness of Amida's compassion and benevolence.

Truly, people everywhere seem to say nothing about the benevolence of Amida Buddha, while focusing only on issues of good and evil. Master Shinran used to say this:

> I know absolutely nothing about good or evil. For if I could know with certainty, as a buddha does, that an act was good, then I would know good. And if I could know thoroughly, as Amida Buddha does, that an act was evil, then I would know evil. This world is as unstable as a burning house, inhabited by human beings consisting of nothing but blind passions; all is empty and foolish, without a grain of truth. Only the nembutsu bestowed by Amida is true.

In reality, when I stop to think about it, I myself as well as others speak nothing but falsehoods. I must mention a sad fact: whenever talking or preaching about the mind with which we say the nembutsu, or the particulars of faith, in order to silence others and drive our point home we attribute to the master words he never said, swearing that he did. We must be especially on our guard against this deplorable tendency.

What I have recorded here are by no means my own thoughts, but as I lack sufficient understanding of the sutras and commentaries and am hardly acquainted with the depths of the scriptures, some parts are bound to be strange. Nevertheless, I have summoned to mind a small portion—barely a hundredth part—of what Master Shinran used to say, and set it down.

How sad it would be if, despite having the rare good fortune of saying the nembutsu, one were not born directly into the true Pure Land but instead lingered on its outer edge! So that there may be no difference in faith among fellow believers who have heard Buddhist truth and studied the teachings, I have taken up my brush with tears in my eyes and set down this record.

I will call it *Tannisho*.[33]

Let it be kept from the eyes of those with no understanding of Buddhism.

[33] *(Lamenting the Deviations)*

An Account of Shinran's Exile[34]

[34] See page 31 for details on Shinran's exile.

During the time when the ex-emperor Go-Toba (1180–1239) was in power,[35] a school of Buddhism based on the other-power nembutsu of the Primal Vow was spread far and wide by Honen. Monks of the temple Kofukuji in Nara despised him for this and petitioned the court, declaring Honen an "enemy of Buddhism." Groundless rumors were spread that his disciples included wicked monks who corrupted public morals. As a result, the following convictions took place.

[35] From around the twelfth century in Japan, real power rested not with the current, but with the retired emperor.

Honen and seven of his disciples were sentenced to exile, and another four disciples were sentenced to death.

Honen was exiled to a place called Hata in Tosa Province.[36] As punishment, he was stripped of his priestly status and assigned the lay name Fujii no Motohiko. He was seventy-six years old.[37]

[36] Modern-day Kochi Prefecture.

[37] The author, Yuien, is incorrect here; Honen was actually seventy-five at this time.

Shinran was exiled to Echigo Province[38] and, as punishment, stripped of his priestly status and assigned the lay name Fujii no Yoshizane. He was thirty-five years old.

[38] Modern-day Niigata Prefecture.

Others who suffered exile include Jomonbo, to Bingo Province;[39] Chosai Zenkobo, to Hoki Province;[40] Kokakubo, to Izu Province;[41] and Gyoku Hohonbo, to Sado Province.[42] Two others, Kosai Jokakubo and Zen'ebo, were also ordered into exile, but the former abbot, Jien, took them into custody and so they were spared.

The people sentenced to exile were the eight named above. Those sentenced to death include the following:

1. Saii Zenshakubo
2. Shoganbo
3. Jurenbo
4. Anrakubo

These sentences were passed by Soncho.

Having received this punishment, Shinran was now neither monk nor layman, so he took as surname the character *toku*, which means "a monk who violates precepts." He formally applied to the court to use this name. It is said that his petition is still kept in the Office of Records. For this reason, after his exile he signed his name "Gutoku[43] Shinran."

Rennyo's Warning[44]

This *Tannisho* is an important sacred text of the True Pure Land School. It should not be read by any who have weak bonds to Amida Buddha, whoever they may be.

—Rennyo,[45] a disciple of Buddha

[39] Modern-day Hiroshima Prefecture.

[40] Modern-day Tottori Prefecture.

[41] Modern-day Shizuoka Prefecture.

[42] Modern-day Niigata Prefecture.

[43] Foolish monk who violates Buddhist precepts.

[44] Appended some one hundred and fifty years after *Tannisho* was written.

[45] Shinran's descendant and a prominent master of True Pure Land Buddhism.

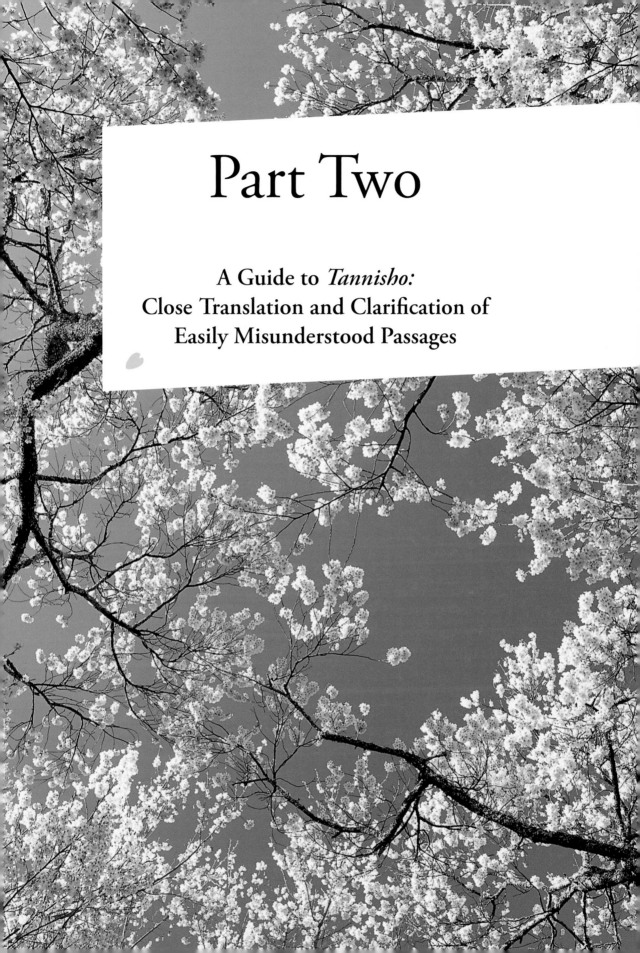

Part Two

A Guide to *Tannisho:*
Close Translation and Clarification of
Easily Misunderstood Passages

Close Translation of
Section I of *Tannisho*

"Saved through the wonder of Amida's Vow, I am certain to achieve birth in the Pure Land": When you believe this, a mind intent on saying the nembutsu arises within you, and in that instant you receive the benefit of being held fast, never to be forsaken. You should know that Amida's Primal Vow does not discriminate between young and old or good and evil; the sole requirement is faith. For the Vow of Amida exists to save sentient beings who are deeply stained with evil and inflamed with passions. Accordingly, once one believes in the Primal Vow, no other good is needed, since there can be no greater good than the nembutsu. Nor is there any need to fear evil, since no evil can block the working of Amida's Primal Vow.

These were his words.

1

How Easy It Is to Misunderstand *Tannisho*

"Saved through the wonder of Amida's Vow, I am certain to achieve birth in the Pure Land": When you believe this, a mind intent on saying the nembutsu arises within you, and in that instant you receive the benefit of being held fast, never to be forsaken.

(*Tannisho*, Section I)

A professor at the prestigious University of Tokyo, someone considered by himself and others to be a Shinran scholar of the first rank, once created a stir by misreading this first section of *Tannisho*. Writing for a high school textbook on Japanese history, he made the following claim: "Shinran taught that if you say the nembutsu out of sincere faith in Amida's salvation, a single recitation is enough to guarantee birth in Paradise."[46] That started the trouble.

Newspapers received letter after letter challenging this assumption. One writer went straight to the heart of the matter: "What if a person dies just after being granted faith in Amida's Vow, without having said the nembutsu even once? Isn't that person assured of Paradise?" People waited eagerly for the great authority to respond, but when he did so, he was disappointingly dismissive: "Whether this answers the question I don't know, but please go back and read *Tannisho* carefully. That is everything."

When we take his advice and read closely, we soon find these words: "When you believe this, a mind intent on saying the nembutsu arises within you, and in that instant you receive the benefit of being held fast, never to be forsaken." The "benefit of being held fast, never to be forsaken" is salvation by Amida with assurance of birth in Paradise. It is conferred when "a mind intent on saying the nembutsu arises within you," in the very instant when you believe. Thus it is obvious that birth in Paradise is assured before the nembutsu is ever spoken.

The professor's stance triggered a lively exchange of opinions,

[46] See copyright page for details on this professor's publications.

with scholars of the True Pure Land School[47] weighing in. They were unsparing in their criticism, declaring his interpretation wrong and in need of revision. Although the professor had remained silent, he soon withdrew his original interpretation and offered this correction: "When the inclination to say the nembutsu arises in you, you at once receive the benefit of being saved by Amida, never to be abandoned."[48] The offending passage in the textbook was rewritten this way: "Shinran taught that salvation comes not by the nembutsu, but by faith alone."

This is an issue that concerns the very core of Shinran's teaching. How could such a fundamental error have come about? Because the professor mistook "When . . . a mind intent on saying the nembutsu arises within you" to mean "when you say the nembutsu once"—even though there is a clear gap between the two. Apparently *Tannisho* is a book that even a leading intellectual and eminent Shinran scholar can get wrong. But this first section, the one in which the message of the entire book is compressed, is crucially important; its meaning must not be misconstrued. How it influences the whole of *Tannisho* cannot be ignored.

[47] The school of Buddhism founded by Shinran.

[48] See copyright page for details on this professor's publications.

2

Amida's Salvation Happens in This Life

"Saved through the wonder of Amida's Vow, I am certain to achieve birth in the Pure Land": When you believe this, a mind intent on saying the nembutsu arises within you, and in that instant you receive the benefit of being held fast, never to be forsaken.

(*Tannisho*, Section I)

Too often, Buddhism in the East is associated mainly with the world after death. And of people who give any thought to Amida's Vow, many think it simply means they are going to Paradise after they die. Shinran rectified these common errors by teaching that Amida's salvation occurs "now," explaining clearly what that salvation is, and showing the true way we can live life to its fullest.

Section I of *Tannisho* is an exceedingly important summary of the heart of Shinran's teaching; all eighteen sections are contained here in essence. It begins by disclosing the ultimate purpose of life, which people throughout history have sought to know: receiving the salvation of Amida—the "benefit of being held fast, never to be forsaken." This is achieved "when . . . a mind intent on saying the nembutsu arises within you." Moreover, the passage goes on to proclaim that Amida's salvation is for all people equally, without discrimination.

Let us dig deeper to learn the timing and nature of salvation. When does it take place? "When you believe this, a mind intent on saying the nembutsu arises within you, and in that instant you receive the benefit of being held fast, never to be forsaken." The passage tells us plainly that salvation happens in this life instantaneously, simultaneously with the occurrence of belief.[49]

And what is the nature of this salvation? The "benefit of being held fast, never to be forsaken." The words are simple and clear, their substance deep and solemn. The "benefit of being held fast, never to be forsaken" is Amida's powerful salvation, but what exactly

[49] In *Teaching, Practice, Faith, Enlightenment*, Shinran uses the word *ichinen* to describe the lightning swiftness of the occurrence of belief: "*Ichinen* [an inconceivably small, irreducible fraction of time] indicates the utmost speed of the onset of faith."

does that mean? This question is crucial. What change does salvation bring about, and how? Unless these points are clarified, *Tannisho* will remain veiled in fog. Let us consider the matter.

The phrase here translated as "held fast, never to be forsaken" means literally "grasping, never abandoning," while "benefit" means "happiness." Salvation is thus the "everlasting happiness of being caught up instantaneously and clasped firmly by Amida, never to be let go." In brief, absolute happiness.

Pascal wrote that the purpose of life is happiness. Indeed, all human activity—even suicide—is driven by the desire for happiness or ease. But the pleasures we seek are mutable, changing in time to pain and sorrow or collapsing and disappearing in a moment. The joys of marriage or a new home—how long will they last? There is no knowing when one's spouse may fall victim to illness or an accident or when love itself may fade, causing the death of all one's hopes. Bereaved wives mourn their husbands; bereaved husbands grieve for their wives; parents rage at their children's betrayal. We all must endure partings, in life as well as in death, from those we love most. When the house it took a lifetime to build is reduced to ashes overnight, or yesterday's happy family is torn apart by a traffic accident or natural disaster, people say, "I never thought this would happen to me." Then they look blankly up at the heavens. Reality is painful and overflowing with tears.

The kind of happiness that is here today and gone tomorrow is full of uncertainty, like treading on thin ice. Even if it continues for a time, it is like a last meal on the eve of execution: the end, when all will be lost, is sadly near. These words from Rennyo[50] sound the warning bell.

[50] Shinran's descendant and a prominent master of True Pure Land Buddhism.

> At the moment of death, nothing one has previously relied on, whether wife and child or money and treasure, will accompany one. At the end of the mountain road of death, one must cross the river all alone.

(*The Letters,* Fascicle 1, Letter 11)

"If I fall ill," a man thinks, "my wife or children will take care of me, and as long as I have money and possessions I needn't worry about food, clothing, or shelter." In this way, people rely on family and possessions in life, but in death there is no such thing to rely on. The journey of death is undertaken naked and alone, all adornments stripped away, and where does it lead?

The shadow of death passing overhead causes joy to fade and

gives rise to the inevitable, agonized question "Why do I live?" At such a time, Shinran's assurance carries the ring of truth: life's true purpose is to gain the happiness of being "held fast, never to be forsaken," which does not change even at death's precipice.

People still live lives of drudgery and torment, chasing happiness that is as fleeting as a candle in the wind. They need to be told of the rock-solid existence of this ultimate happiness granted by Amida. Once this ultimate happiness is theirs, people can enjoy complete joy and satisfaction anytime and anywhere, savoring the lasting pleasure of having achieved life's cherished dream.

Here is Shinran's joyous testimony:

> How genuine, the true words of Amida that embrace us and never forsake us, the absolute doctrine that is peerless and transcendent!

(Teaching, Practice, Faith, Enlightenment)

This is a cry of astonished joy as Shinran experiences the truth of Amida's salvation: His life fraught with suffering has been instantly transformed without any change in quality or quantity, bringing him from eternal darkness into absolute happiness. It is this Shinran who described for us in detail the supreme truth of Amida's salvation, the truth that holds us fast and never lets us go.

3

"The Sole Requirement Is Faith"

You should know that Amida's Primal Vow does not discriminate between young and old or good and evil; the sole requirement is faith.

(*Tannisho*, Section I)

"Everyone who says the nembutsu will be saved": there is a widespread, mistaken belief that this, in a nutshell, is what Shinran taught. The above passage from Section I sets straight not only this common error but many others pertaining to the whole of *Tannisho*. These words of Shinran truly are of boundless significance. Let us examine the messages they contain.

First, the Vow "does not discriminate between young and old or good and evil." Just as the sea refuses no river, there is no discrimination of any kind in Amida's salvation. Old and young, those whom we judge to be good or evil—all alike are saved equally through the Vow.

Second, despite the above reassurance of nondiscrimination, the statement ends with a stern reminder: "You should know that … the sole requirement is faith." Some may interpret this to mean that like other religious leaders, Shinran preached the importance of believing in some higher power. What he means here by "faith," however, is something fundamentally different, something truly enlightening.

In general, praying for favors such as riches, restoration of health, protection from disaster, or the well-being of one's family is seen an expression of faith. Most people conceive of religious faith as believing in a deity with deep, unquestioning conviction. Yet if you think about it, such belief is unnecessary if there is absolutely no room for doubt. No one looking out the window at a beautiful blue sky says he "believes" it's a nice day; no one who has suffered third-degree burns says he "believes" fire is hot. When something is so clear that there can be no doubt, we say rather that we "know" it to be so. We only say we believe something when there is, in fact, some underlying doubt. Faith in the general sense means clinging to a belief in the face of continuing doubt and uncertainty. But the faith that Shinran calls essential to salvation is nothing like this.

What Shinran means by faith is the vanishing of all doubt concerning Amida's Vow. Let us use another analogy to clarify the difference. When an airplane runs into severe turbulence and shakes violently, the pilot may announce, "It's all right, folks. There's nothing to worry about." Passengers' nagging doubts and fears will be put to rest only when the plane makes a safe landing. Similarly, doubts about a promised rescue vanish when the rescue takes place, and doubts about a promised gift vanish when the gift is handed over. In the same way, doubts concerning Amida's Vow to grant absolute happiness vanish the moment a person is "held fast, never to be forsaken" and actually enters into that happiness.

Such faith is not something anyone can generate on his own or talk himself into. When it arises, it does so solely as the gift of Amida. The faith bestowed by Amida is categorically different from all other faith because it is not beset by doubt. This faith, called "other-power faith," is peerless and transcendent. Shinran never taught anything but other-power faith, and this is why the essence of his teachings is known as "salvation by faith alone."

Here are two representative statements from other writings of his:

> The true cause of Nirvana[51] is faith alone.

> Faith alone is the cause of true settlement.[52]

Nirvana may be paraphrased as "birth in the Pure Land," while "true settlement" means "becoming clearly settled in this life to attain buddhahood."

Rennyo also made this unequivocal statement in one of his *Letters*:[53]

> The essence of founder Shinran's lifelong teaching is faith alone and nothing else.

In his last testament he wrote:

> Ah! My constant wish, morning and night, is that everyone may obtain faith while still alive.

[51] Nirvana: The same level of enlightenment as Amida Buddha.

(Teaching, Practice, Faith, Enlightenment)

(Hymn of True Faith)

[52] True settlement: Salvation by Amida in this life; absolute happiness.

[53] *The Letters*: A collection of letters written by Rennyo, consisting of eighty letters in five fascicles.

(Fascicle 2, Letter 3)

(Fascicle 4, Letter 15)

Short though it is, this first section that summarizes all of *Tannisho* refers again and again to faith:

> "When you believe this . . ."
> "Once one believes in the Primal Vow . . ."
> "You should know that . . . the sole requirement is faith."

Clearly "faith" is of key importance in Shinran's teachings. Let it be remembered that any attempt to understand *Tannisho* in ignorance of other-power faith is as likely to succeed as climbing a tree in search of fish.

4

"No Need for Good, No Fear of Evil": What Does This Really Mean?

Once one believes in the Primal Vow, no other good is needed, since there can be no greater good than the nembutsu. Nor is there any need to fear evil, since no evil can block the working of Amida's Primal Vow.

(*Tannisho*, Section I)

The passage above is particularly subject to misinterpretation. All too often, people take it to mean that as long as they recite the nembutsu, they don't need to do any other good works to be saved by Amida's Vow, since there is no greater good than the nembutsu; they further misinterpret the passage as saying that because Amida's Vow has power over all evil, they don't need to be afraid of any evil they may commit. Even in Shinran's time, people evidently interpreted these words to suit themselves and committed evil without concern, for Shinran issued frequent warnings against what was called "remorseless indulgence." Here are two examples from *Lamp for the Latter Age*, a collection of his letters and sayings:

> You must not do what should not be done, think what should not be thought, or say what should not be said, thinking that you can go to the Pure Land anyway.

> You are apparently saying that because we are by nature a mass of blind passions, it cannot be helped if we yield to desire and do what should not be done, say what should not be said, or think what should not be thought; that indeed we might as well follow our every inclination. This is pitiful in the extreme. It is like offering wine to a man who is still drunk, or telling someone still with poison in his system, "There is an antidote, so take all the poison you like." Such a thing is beyond the pale.

These passages convey his tears of sadness and anger at the difficulty of having the truth properly understood.

Then what is the true meaning of the passage in question from Section I?

"No other good is needed." This means that one who is saved by Amida's Vow has no mind to perform good works *in order to ensure his birth in the Pure Land*, since he has the great satisfaction of knowing for certain that his birth there is assured through the nembutsu granted by Amida. A person cured by a wonder drug has no mind to seek any other medicine; new medicine is needed only if the cure is incomplete. In the same way, a person who is saved has no possible need to do good works in order to be saved. Feeling such a need amounts to proof that one is not saved.

"Nor is there any need to fear evil." To consider what this means, let us examine other words of Shinran's.

> I am incapable of doing any good at all, and so hell is my eternal dwelling-place.

(*Tannisho*, Section II)

Once it was revealed to Shinran that he was the worst of sinners, with no possible destination but hell, he could no longer fear any evil. His situation was similar to that of a prisoner who, his death sentence finalized by the Supreme Court, has no judgment left to fear.

One saved by Amida's Vow is awakened to the inconceivable world of "twofold revelation"[54]: it is revealed to him simultaneously that beyond doubt he will go to hell for eternity, and that beyond doubt he will go to Paradise for eternity. It is only natural that one in this state of mind would declare "Nor is there any need to fear evil." Anyone who feels anxious and fearful at the evil he commits has not experienced the revelation that he is an evildoer destined beyond any doubt for hell.

The passage quoted at the beginning of this chapter is a straightforward expression of the "unnamable, inexplicable, inconceivable faith" Shinran received from Amida, a faith that is "peerless and transcendent." Most of the errors of interpretation that Shinran corrects in *Lamp for the Latter Age* could never have arisen in any who had direct knowledge of this great sea of faith.[55] Shinran's deep sorrow is evident.

Because *Tannisho* is so easily misunderstood, Rennyo issued a stern warning against sharing it indiscriminately.

[54] Faith that is beyond ordinary comprehension, in which the self that cannot be saved and the self that is saved are simultaneously and continuously revealed without a shadow of doubt.

[55] Other-power faith.

Close Translation of
Section II of *Tannisho*

Each of you has come seeking me, crossing the borders of more than
ten provinces at the risk of your life, with one thing only in mind: to
ask the path to birth in the land of utmost bliss. But if you imagine
that I have knowledge of some path to birth other than the nembutsu,
or that I know of other scriptures, you are greatly in error.

In that case you should go to the southern capital or the northern
peak, where there are many eminent scholars, and ask in detail about
the essence of birth in the Pure Land.

As for me, I simply trust in the teaching of my revered teacher:
"Only say the nembutsu and be saved by Amida Buddha." There is
nothing more to it than this.

I do not know in the least whether saying the nembutsu is truly the
seed for my birth in the Pure Land or whether it is an act for which I
must fall into hell. Even if I have been deceived by Master Honen and
fall into hell for saying the nembutsu, I will have no regrets. The reason is that if I could attain buddhahood by devoting myself to other
practices, but fell into hell for saying the nembutsu, I would feel regret
at having been deceived; but I am incapable of doing any good at all,
and so hell is my eternal dwelling-place.

Given that Amida's Primal Vow is true, the sermons of Śākyamuni
Buddha cannot be empty words. Given that the Buddha's sermons are
true, the commentaries of Shan-tao cannot be empty. If Shan-tao's
commentaries are true, can the sayings of Honen be false? If Honen's
sayings are true, how could what I, Shinran, say be false?

In the end, this is my faith. Beyond this, whether to accept and
believe in the nembutsu or whether to reject it is for each of you to
decide.

These were his words.

5

Does Other-Power Mean That We Sit Back and Do Nothing?

Each of you has come seeking me, crossing the borders of more than ten provinces at the risk of your life, with one thing only in mind: to ask the path to birth in the land of utmost bliss.

(*Tannisho*, Section II)

Many people would say they know good from evil, and feel no pressing need to hear Buddhism. Even among those who listen to Buddhism, few realize that Buddhist teaching concerns the crucial matter of birth and death[56] and how to resolve it. Irresponsible remarks abound: salvation is based on other-power faith; we're all going to Paradise when we die anyway; there's no need to listen earnestly. Voices like these are heard on all sides.

But the second section of *Tannisho* contains an account of a harrowing confrontation between Shinran and people who risked their lives to hear true Buddhist teaching. Some background understanding is necessary, so let us first briefly examine the course of Shinran's life.

Shinran was born in Kyoto at the end of the twelfth century, just before the tumultuous Genpei War.[57] He lost his father at four and his mother at eight. Astonished by the realization that he, too, was mortal and would be next to die, at age nine he applied to and was inducted into the Tendai school[58] of Buddhism at its head temple atop Mount Hiei in Kyoto.

Tendai monks sought to follow Buddhist precepts and fight off worldly passions[59] in order to achieve enlightenment. For the next twenty years, Shinran's life of rigorous ascetic training on Mount Hiei was a constant struggle with his blind passions. Try as he would to subdue the raging dogs of his passions, they never left him alone. He mused, "The winds of mortality may blow this way at any time. If I go on as I am, I cannot escape eternal suffering."

[56] The crucial matter of birth and death: Whether one will sink into an eternity of suffering or gain everlasting happiness.

[57] An epic conflict (1180–85) between two powerful military clans.

[58] A school of Buddhism founded by Saicho (767–822) in Japan. It teaches practices following the Lotus Sutra.

[59] The same as blind passions: Lust, anger, jealousy, and other delusions of the heart that trouble and torment us.

Feeling the urgency of his plight as death's shadow crept ever closer, he lost faith in the teachings of Tendai Buddhism and resolved to leave the order.

Wondering if there was to be no salvation for him, no great teacher to show him the way, Shinran wandered the streets of Kyoto like a sleepwalker. Eventually he ran into a friend from Mount Hiei named Seikaku, through whose offices he met Honen, founder of the Pure Land School and a prominent man of the times. Day in and day out Shinran devoted himself to listening to Honen's sermons, and one day, in a split second, he was saved by Amida Buddha's Vow. He was then twenty-nine, and Honen was sixty-nine.

Oppression of the Pure Land School

Followers of Honen increased rapidly, their numbers swelling to include not only samurai and common people but also scholars of the Tendai, Shingon, Zen, and other schools of Buddhism, as well as members of the aristocracy and nobility. Fearful of the surge in popularity of the Pure Land School, the other schools felt a sense of crisis. They could not sit back and idly watch as their supporters in the nobility and aristocracy turned to Honen. Eventually they banded together and took the unheard-of step of directly petitioning the emperor.

In 1207 the Pure Land School was dissolved, teaching of the nembutsu was prohibited, and eight people, including Honen and Shinran, were banished. Four of Honen's disciples, including Juren and Anraku, were executed. Shinran too was originally scheduled for execution, but thanks to the intervention of the former regent Kujo Kanezane, his sentence was commuted to exile in the northeastern province of Echigo.[60] He was then thirty-five years old. Honen was banished in the opposite direction, to Tosa[61] on the island of Shikoku.

Collusion between political and religious authorities led to this brutal oppression never before seen in the history of Japanese Buddhism. The persecution is referred to at the end of *Tannisho*.

[60] Modern-day Niigata Prefecture.

[61] Modern-day Kochi Prefecture.

From Echigo to Kanto and Back to Kyoto

Five years later, in the snow and cold of Echigo, Shinran received word of his pardon. He moved on to the eastern Kanto district, setting up a simple hut in the village of Inada in Hitachi[62] where for the next twenty years he devoted himself single-mindedly to teaching Amida's Primal Vow. After turning sixty, he returned to his native Kyoto and gradually began to concentrate on writing. Most of his copious writings were done after the age of seventy-six.

After Shinran left Kanto, a number of events sowed confusion among his followers there. Agitated by the profound upheaval in their faith, several of them resolved to make the perilous journey to Kyoto in order to meet directly with the master and ascertain the truth.

The journey would take a month or more. On the way they would cross over mountains, ford rivers, and be threatened by murderous thieves and bandits lurking everywhere. There was no knowing if they would return alive. Each one who made the trip did so truly "at the risk of [his] life," determined to hear the truth of Buddhism no matter what the cost, just as Shinran had exhorted. All their lives, they remained faithful to the ever-present voice of Shinran.

[62] Modern-day Ibaraki Prefecture.

The Path to Birth in Paradise

Section II begins with Shinran's blunt remark to the believers: "Each of you has come seeking me . . . at the risk of your life, with one thing only in mind: to ask the path to birth in the land of utmost bliss." Clearly, during his twenty years in the Kanto area this path was all that he had taught.

What is the "path to birth in the land of utmost bliss"? It is the Vow of Amida Buddha to all humanity: "I will enable you to be born in the Pure Land without fail."

The followers' state of mind is fully understandable as, their faith in the Vow shaken, they staked their lives on a trip to attain the fulfillment of knowing that they could go to the Pure Land without fail.

Determination to Hear Buddhist Teaching

> Though the universe
> should become a sea of flames,
> he who crosses it to hear the Name of Amida
> will achieve everlasting salvation.

(Hymns on the Pure Land)

This hymn by Shinran means that if you keep on listening to Buddhism "through hell and high water" and you are saved by Amida, you are certain to achieve radiant, eternal bliss. Rennyo's teaching was identical:

> Buddhism must be heard
> even if it means fighting one's way
> through raging flames;
> then what hindrance can there be
> in rain or wind or snow?

Rennyo further offers this instruction on priorities.

> Buddhism must be listened to by setting aside the world's affairs. Thinking that one should listen to Buddhist law when not occupied with the world's affairs is shallow.

(The Words of Rennyo Heard and Recorded During His Lifetime)

In other words, Buddhism is so important that it must be apprehended even if it means dropping all our work. The assumption that it is enough to fit Buddhism in between other things in life shows a sad lack of understanding. Here Rennyo describes means of living as "the world's affairs." Given that resolving the crucial matter of birth and death is our true purpose in life, one can only marvel at the aptness of this pithy phrase.

Yet where on earth can these teachings of Shinran and Rennyo be heard today? Almost nowhere. No matter how carefully one peruses Section II—or indeed all of *Tannisho*—the main point will regrettably be missed unless one is aware that Buddhist truth must be heard even at the risk of one's life.

6

"Only Say the Nembutsu": The Meaning of "Only"

As for me, I simply trust in the teaching of my revered teacher: "Only say the nembutsu and be saved by Amida Buddha." There is nothing more to it than this.

(*Tannisho*, Section II)

Misunderstanding is rampant regarding what is meant by "Only say the nembutsu and be saved by Amida Buddha." Many people take this to mean "Only utter 'Namu Amida Butsu'"—the syllables that compose the nembutsu—and so they assume that Shinran was saved just by reciting the nembutsu. This is an error based on superficial knowledge. As we have already seen, Shinran's teachings stress that salvation comes from faith, and are for this reason often summed up as "salvation by faith alone." Section I of *Tannisho*, for example, states unequivocally that for salvation "the sole requirement is faith." Rennyo also testified to this point many times. Here is a small sample from his *Letters*:

For birth in the Pure Land, all that is needed is other-power faith alone.

(Fascicle 2, Letter 5)

With other-power faith alone comes birth in the Pure Land.

(Fascicle 2, Letter 7)

Only attain other-power faith, and without a doubt you will be born in Paradise.

(Fascicle 2, Letter 14)

Best known of all is this declaration:

All his life, Shinran taught "salvation by faith alone."

(Fascicle 5, Letter 10)

Then what does "only say the nembutsu" really mean? The word "only" expresses amazement at Amida's unconditional, perfect, and free salvation.

Human beings have an innate resistance to the truth about themselves. Being confronted with our evil nature that dooms us to hell upsets us less than the loss of ten dollars. Told in no uncertain terms that life has an end, one that may come before tomorrow, we are unfazed, convinced we'll be all right. In the same way, when told that Amida saves us as we are, we rejoice less than we would if we were handed a dollar bill. If we take ourselves to task for this insensitivity and try to listen earnestly to the message of Buddhism, we find deep within ourselves the mind of a stolid ox, so glazed over, drowsy, and vacant that it has no interest in hearing a single word. In Shinran's striking phrase, this is "the mind of a corpse"—that is, a mind as unresponsive as a corpse.

Even when we grumble, "I'll never listen to Buddhism in a million years!" Amida responds, "I have fully known this about you all along; entrust yourself to me as you are." To anyone who hears this call, such compassion is nothing short of astonishing.

The meaning of "only" in "only say the nembutsu" is this: Knowing full well that you can have no destination other than hell, entrust the crucial question of your ultimate fate[63] to Amida, leaving all in his hands. This is the unnamable, inexplicable, inconceivable "only," the silent voice that can and will reach the ears of everyone, even the stone deaf. It expresses other-power faith, in which the believer and Amida Buddha gain life together at the same time.

[63] Eternal suffering or eternal bliss.

Thus "say the nembutsu" means to utter the nembutsu in an outpouring of gratitude rising from the joy of salvation. In *Hymn of True Faith*, Shinran explains the meaning of the nembutsu this way:

> Only saying the Name of Amida constantly,
> respond in gratitude to the Vow of great compassion.

In other words, once we receive other-power faith we respond gratefully to Amida's benevolence, filled ceaselessly with the nembutsu. *The Letters* of Rennyo contains more detailed explanations:

> After one is saved by Amida Buddha, the recitation of the Name is an expression of infinite gratitude to Amida for settling one's birth in the Pure Land. This should be understood.

(Fascicle 5, Letter 10)

To be "held fast, never forsaken" means that one is saved by Amida and will never be cast aside. Such a person is said to have gained faith. The one who has gained faith repeats "Namu Amida Butsu" asleep or awake, standing or sitting; this nembutsu should be understood as an expression of gratitude for Amida's salvation.

(Fascicle 1, Letter 7)

In *Tannisho*, the nembutsu is identified in Section I as an expression of gratitude to Amida Buddha rising out of a "mind intent on saying the nembutsu" and spoken in joy at having "receive[d] the benefit of being held fast, never to be forsaken" (i.e., at having gained faith).

The true meaning of "only say the nembutsu" must be understood in the light of Shinran's teaching that faith alone brings salvation and the nembutsu is spoken in gratitude. Otherwise "the sublime, all-complete teaching [that is] the essence of truth" will be lost.

7

The Real Meaning of Shinran's "I Do Not Know in the Least"

I do not know in the least whether saying the nembutsu is truly the seed for my birth in the Pure Land or whether it is an act for which I must fall into hell.

(*Tannisho*, Section II)

Some people unfamiliar with Shinran's teachings deride this statement, declaring that it shows the man literally had no idea whether saying the nembutsu would land him in paradise or in hell. Others chastise him for giving no satisfaction to those who came to him for answers at the risk of their lives. They have it entirely wrong.

It is indisputable that Shinran definitively declared the nembutsu said without a remnant of doubt in Amida's Vow the "path to birth in the land of utmost bliss." He taught that there is no way to the Pure Land but by the working of this nembutsu that arises from faith. As proof, let us offer several quotations from his writings that make this crystal clear.

> Attaining buddhahood through the working of the other-power nembutsu:[64] this is true Buddhism.
> Myriad good acts of self-power are all a provisional gate.
> Without knowing the expedient and the real, the true and the provisional,
> One cannot know the true Pure Land of Amida.

[64] See Glossary, "other-power nembutsu."

(*Hymns of the Pure Land*)

True Buddhist teaching holds that the enlightenment of a buddha —the highest of fifty-two levels of enlightenment—is attained through the working of the other-power nembutsu. Self-power Buddhism is an expedient means of leading all sentient beings to the truth.

When we say "Namu Amida Butsu,"
the benefits we gain in this world are boundless.
The evil that causes the endless wheel of suffering[65] disappears,
and we are spared untimely death and the torments we
    deserve.

Reciting the nembutsu brings an end to the evil that is the ultimate cause of the suffering we have long endured, sparing us the calamities and premature death that we richly deserve and allowing us to live now and forever in perfect happiness.

Those who slander the nembutsu
fall into Avici Hell[66]
to suffer great pain and torment without cease
for eighty thousand kalpas, it is taught.

The sutras teach that those who disparage the supremely precious nembutsu will suffer terrible consequences. Such people are fated to fall into Avici Hell, the worst of all worlds, a place of unremitting suffering where for eighty thousand kalpas—a mind-bendingly long time—they must endure extreme agony without cease. Shinran further explains in *Teaching, Practice, Faith, Enlightenment* that while the bodhisattva[67] Miroku[68] will not attain buddhahood for another 5.67 billion years, "all those of the nembutsu[69] have attained the diamond faith[70] bestowed by Amida and will therefore, at the moment of death, attain absolute Nirvana." Unlike Miroku, those of the nembutsu attain the enlightenment of a buddha even as their life on this earth ends.

For twenty years in the Kanto region, Shinran taught nothing but the nembutsu of Amida's Vow.[71] Yet after his return to Kyoto, a number of events took place to shake the faith of those he left behind. One was the blasphemous insistence of the monk Nichiren[72] that anyone who said the nembutsu would go to Avici Hell, the hell of greatest suffering. Nichiren stirred agitation throughout Kanto by fanatically spreading this lie.

Perceiving what was on the minds of those who, driven by doubt and desperation, had come such a long distance to hear the truth directly from his lips, Shinran was sick at heart. After all he had taught them, now they sat before him afraid that the act of saying the nembutsu might land them in hell. He voiced his grieved disappointment by saying bluntly, "How should I know!" The bitterness of this declaration is painfully apparent. Given the

(Hymns of the Pure Land)

[65] Endless wheel of suffering: Transmigration. Endlessly repeated brth and death in myriad life forms.

(Hymns on the Three Ages)

[66] The worst of all hells. A realm of ceaseless suffering.

[67] A seeker of true happiness; one striving to attain the enlightenment of a buddha.

[68] Miroku, "the Buddha of the future," is at the highest spiritual stage but one, just short of buddhahood.

[69] Those who say the nembutsu on having received salvation from Amida Buddha.

[70] Diamond faith: Faith that is impervious to any attack.

[71] The nembutsu said without a remnant of doubt in Amida's Vow.

[72] Founder of the Nichiren sect (1222–82). A vocal opponent of Pure Land beliefs.

circumstances, no response could have been more appropriate. In daily life, when asked a glaringly obvious question, anyone might reply that way, biting back more irritated words. Even when the answer is perfectly clear, if pushed too far we are apt to thrust the questioner off with some such disavowal. By no means was Shinran leading his followers on, affecting ignorance so that they would conclude it was all right for them not to know whether the nembutsu would lead to paradise or hell, since even he couldn't say. Far from it!

Tannisho also contains these famous words: "Only the nembutsu is true." Shinran, for whom the question of whether saying the nembutsu would lead to paradise or hell was not an issue, gave the clearest possible expression to his vibrant, steadfast conviction. It is easy to imagine the band of followers returning to Kanto in high spirits, brimming with joy at their encounter with the holy man's supreme confidence.

8

Because Amida's Vow Is True

Given that Amida's Primal Vow is true, the sermons of Śākyamuni Buddha cannot be empty words. Given that the Buddha's sermons are true, the commentaries of Shan-tao cannot be empty. If Shan-tao's commentaries are true, can the sayings of Honen be false? If Honen's sayings are true, how could what I, Shinran, say be false? (*Tannisho*, Section II)

Surprisingly many people misread the opening of this passage as "If we suppose that Amida's Primal Vow is true ..." But for Shinran, there was no truth in this world apart from the Vow of Amida. Elsewhere he exclaimed in joy:

How genuine, the true words of Amida that embrace us and never forsake us, the absolute doctrine that is peerless and transcendent!

(Teaching, Practice, Faith, Enlightenment)

In this world as fleeting and unstable as a burning house, inhabited by human beings beset by worldly passions, all is idleness and foolishness, utterly devoid of truth. Only the nembutsu is true.

(Tannisho, Epilogue)

"Only the nembutsu is true" is another way of saying "Only Amida's Vow is true." Shinran's faith in the truth of the Vow is crystal clear: all of his writings are full of exultation in it, and it is indeed the starting-point for all his teachings. It is unthinkable that he would refer to the truth of the Vow in the conditional mood, as a hypothetical case.

Here Shinran is definitely declaring, "Because Amida's Primal Vow is true." With that as a given, it follows that the sayings of Śākyamuni, Shan-tao, and Honen, all of whom preached only the Vow, must be true; therefore Shinran, too, who has faithfully transmitted their teachings, can be no liar. This is supreme confidence.

Some may pause here and scratch their heads. After all, to the men from the Kanto area, it was precisely the words of Shinran that carried the most authority, and it was precisely Amida's Vow about which they were unsure. They believed in it because of Shinran's assurances that the teachings of Honen, Shan-tao, and Śākyamuni were all true. Even so, to settle the doubts in their minds, Shinran took the truth of Amida's Primal Vow as his starting point, offering no proof or explanation. It might reasonably be asked whether his approach was not backwards.

For Shinran, saved in accord with Amida's Vow, the clearest, most undeniable truth in the world was the Primal Vow of Amida Buddha. The serenity of his faith can be likened to the moon reflected in the sea: no matter how the billows rage, that moon will never be lost, never be destroyed, never vanish away. Because Shinran had a direct connection with the Primal Vow, even if the teachings of Śākyamuni, Shan-tao, and Honen had all proved false, his faith in the Vow could never waver.

"Given that Amida's Primal Vow is true": Shinran's ability to make this flat, unhesitating assertion came solely from the clear working in him of other-power faith.

Close Translation of
Section III of *Tannisho*

Even a good person will be born in the Pure Land; how much more so an evil person! This is so, yet people commonly say, "Even an evil person attains birth; all the more so will a good person." This statement seems well founded at first, but it runs counter to the intention of the Primal Vow of other-power.

This is because people who seek to do good through self-power do not rely wholeheartedly on other-power and are therefore not in accord with the Primal Vow. If people overturn the mind of self-power and rely on other-power, they will attain birth in the land of true fulfillment.

It is impossible for us, who are filled with blind passions, to free ourselves from the cycle of birth and death through any practice whatever. Taking pity on our state, Amida made the Vow with the real intent of ensuring the evil person's attainment of buddhahood. Therefore, evil persons who rely on other-power are the very ones who have obtained the true cause of birth.

Accordingly he said, "Even a good person will be born, to say nothing of a person who is evil."

These were his words.

9

"If Even a Good Person Will Attain Salvation, All the More So Will an Evil Person"

Even a good person will be born in the Pure Land; how much more so an evil person!

(Tannisho, Section III)

These well-known words from *Tannisho* are, it is said, the most famous words in the history of Japanese thought. Their content is so sensational that they have also given rise to enormous misunderstanding.

The assertions that "even" a good person can go to the Pure Land and an evil person is all the more likely to be saved appear to lead naturally to the conclusion that the more evil a person does in his lifetime, the greater his chances of salvation. In fact, some followers embraced the idea of "licensed evil" and performed acts of malice, giving rise to the criticism that Shinran's teaching encouraged vice. This deep-rooted misinterpretation lingers even now.

The only way to set the record straight is to delve into Shinran's understanding of a "good person" and an "evil person." Otherwise the most enthusiastic reading of Section III, and indeed of the whole of *Tannisho*, will lead only to empty learning, not true understanding.

We constantly categorize others as good or evil, basing our judgments on common sense, law, ethics, and morals. But by an "evil person" Shinran meant something completely different from just an ordinary criminal or "bad guy." It is a profoundly serious meaning that offers a transformative view of human nature. Section II of *Tannisho* quotes Shinran as saying, "I am incapable of doing any good at all, and so hell is my eternal dwelling-place." The truth of this confession does not apply only to Shinran. It is the unfeigned truth about every person who has ever lived, in all times and places, as both *Teaching, Practice, Faith, Enlightenment* and *Tannisho* repeat often and in strong terms.

> The sea of all sentient beings, from time immemorial until this very day and hour, is polluted with evil and lacking in a mind of purity; it is false and deceitful, lacking in a mind of truth.

(Teaching, Practice, Faith, Enlightenment)

All people, from those in remote antiquity to those who will be born in the far-distant future, are filled with wickedness, falsehoods, and drivel; the human heart contains not an ounce of truth. Not only that, we humans are brazen and shameless, impenitent toward others and unashamed in our own heart. We have no hope of salvation for all eternity.

The following passage from the second half of Section III drives the point home:

> It is impossible for us, who are filled with blind passions, to free ourselves from the cycle of birth and death through any practice whatever. Taking pity on our state, Amida made the Vow with the real intent of ensuring the evil person's attainment of buddhahood.

It was precisely because Amida Buddha saw that people are all a mass of blind passions, evil without a hope of salvation for all eternity, that he vowed to save them. Herein lies the true value of the Primal Vow of Amida.

Shinran's "evil person" thus refers to all humanity, whose evil nature Amida Buddha unerringly perceived. "An evil person" is simply another way of saying "a human being."

What then does Shinran mean by "a good person"? This is someone who seeks to do good in order to be saved, or who recites the nembutsu in hopes of gaining salvation. Because such a person believes himself capable of doing good if he only tries, and imagines he can keep on saying the nembutsu throughout his life, Shinran says that he is a person who does "good through self-power." And because such a one doubts the power of Amida's Vow, which was made precisely for the evil person incapable of doing any good at all, Shinran also uses the expression a "good person of doubting mind."

Such a person, one who is immersed in self-power with no intention of casting aside prudence and discretion and entrusting himself or herself fully to Amida, cannot be an object of the Vow. This point is explained in Section III as follows:

> This is because people who seek to do good through self-power do not rely wholeheartedly on other-power and are therefore not in accord with the Primal Vow.

And yet Amida has vowed to break through the conceit of such a "good" person—one whose wrong views and arrogance blind him to his own evil nature—and cause him to be born in the Pure Land. It is because Amida will induce even a "person who does good through self-power" to be saved that Shinran said, "Even a good person will be born in the Pure Land; how much more so an evil person!"

The notion that the more evil we do, the more likely we are to be saved, or that evildoing is the true cause of salvation, has no place in Shinran's teaching. For all people, good and bad alike, Shinran emphasized nothing but other-power faith, which is the gift of Amida Buddha. The following two passages from Section III are unequivocal:

> If people overturn the mind of self-power and rely on other-power, they will attain birth in the land of true fulfillment.

In other words, it is by casting aside the self-power which doubts the efficacy of the Primal Vow, and gaining other-power faith instead, that we can be born in the true Pure Land.

> Evil persons who rely on other-power are the very ones who have obtained the true cause of birth.

Both passages above contain the expression "rely on other-power," which also occurs in sacred writings by Shinran's own hand:

> Relying on the Primal Vow of other-power and leaving aside self-power: this is "faith alone."

(Notes on "Essentials of Faith Alone")

Here Shinran writes "relying on . . . other-power," and in *Tannisho* we read "if people . . . rely on other-power." Rennyo uses the phrase "relying on Amida." All of these passages refer to nothing but other-power faith, which alone brings salvation.

Section III of *Tannisho*, while drawing an apparent distinction between good and evil, shows that the entire focus of Amida's salvation is other-power faith. This focus is also clear from the great declaration in Section I that Amida's salvation "does not discriminate between young and old or good and evil; the sole requirement is faith." This surely is the essential point in *Tannisho* that must be stressed and brought to people's attention.

Close Translation of
Section IV of *Tannisho*

Concerning compassion, there is a difference between the way of the sages and the Pure Land way. Compassion in the way of the sages means to pity, love, and nurture others; however, it is all but impossible to help others as one would wish. Pure Land compassion lies in saying the nembutsu, quickly attaining buddhahood, and then, with a mind of great love and compassion, freely working for the benefit of all sentient beings.

In this life, however much love and sympathy we feel, it is difficult to save others as we wish, and so such compassion remains unfulfilled. Therefore, saying the nembutsu is alone the great mind of thorough-going compassion.

These were his words.

10

The Real Meaning of "Quickly Attaining Buddhahood"

Pure Land compassion lies in saying the nembutsu, quickly attaining buddhahood, and then, with a mind of great love and compassion, freely working for the benefit of all sentient beings.   (*Tannisho*, Section IV)

The phrase "quickly attaining buddhahood" in the passage above has been criticized as meaning "quickly dying." Those who voice this criticism doubtless do so in full awareness of Shinran's consistent teaching that the enlightenment of a buddha is obtained only on being born in the Pure Land after death. If "quickly attaining buddhahood" is taken literally, then it would follow that "Pure Land compassion" cannot be achieved unless we quickly die. In that case, the criticism would be entirely justified.

Yet to equate "quickly attaining buddhahood" with "quickly dying" is obviously in error, since not everyone attains buddhahood when they die. Only one who has met with Amida's salvation in this life and become assured of attaining buddhahood upon dying can be born in the Pure Land and achieve supreme enlightenment. This was Shinran's lifelong teaching. So it is clear that "quickly attaining buddhahood" means "quickly *gaining assurance of* attaining buddhahood": in other words, quickly encountering Amida's salvation now, during this lifetime.

Only after attaining supreme enlightenment in the Pure Land can anyone freely benefit other sentient beings from a heart of great love and compassion. But what happens in the meantime, after one is saved by Amida and becomes able to achieve buddhahood? Shinran expressed the state of mind of such a person in these words:

The grace of Amida's great compassion
I must repay, though I work myself to the bone.
The grace of the teachers who led me
I must repay, though I wear myself to bits.

(Song of Amida's Grace and Virtue)

The benevolence of Amida Buddha and the debt of gratitude owed to teachers of the Vow can never be fully repaid. Not even sacrificing oneself would suffice. All anyone can do is weep at his own laziness for not making a particle of recompense.

The heart brimming with gratitude that knows no bounds cannot help imitating the compassion of the Pure Land. When Shinran was twenty-nine, he obtained other-power faith and so became assured of achieving buddhahood. From then on, with tears of gratitude, "mindful solely of the depth of Amida's benevolence and paying no mind to others' derision,"[73] he lived a life of extraordinary devotion and gratitude to Amida—a life that bore no trace of the negative, indolent mindset that would put off saving others until after death.

[73] From the postscript to his major work, *Teaching, Practice, Faith, Enlightenment.*

Let us examine the sixty-one years of Shinran's life from the time of his salvation until his death at age ninety.

At the age of thirty-one he broke with Buddhist monastic tradition by beginning to eat fish and by taking a wife, acts which were unprecedented ways of conveying Amida's great desire for the salvation of all people. Nevertheless, in so doing he aroused a storm of controversy and was subjected to a barrage of denunciations as a madman, a devil, and a depraved monk. His breaking of these taboos led directly to his later banishment.

Normally meek, Shinran fought distortions of Buddhist truth with unswerving resolve, willing even to forfeit his life if need be. This fierceness led him often to instigate heated debates with his fellow disciples. The most noteworthy of these clashes are known to posterity as the Three Great Debates, one of which is mentioned in the postscript to *Tannisho.*

At the age of thirty-five Shinran was exiled to Echigo, as is well known, but few know the real reason why. The main reason was his insistence on Śākyamuni's teaching that one must leave aside all other buddhas, bodhisattvas, and gods, and turn only to Amida[74]—the teaching that was the very reason for Śākyamuni's appearance in this world. Shinran's rejection of all other deities earned him the particular wrath of those in power. Many at the time considered Japan the "land of the gods," and the rejection of

[74] *Ikko sennen muryoju butsu*: "[Offer] single-minded devotion to the Buddha of Infinite Life." From the Larger Sutra of Infinite Life.

these traditional deities was seen as a despicable heresy that would turn society upside down. Accordingly, the wrath of the highest authorities and those in league with them came down on Shinran, and he received a sentence of death, narrowly commuted to exile.

But as the saying goes, "though the wind blows from all sides, the mountain remains firm." Shinran lashed out at the self-delusion of his attackers with these scathing words:

> From emperor to retainer, they rebel against Buddha's teachings and trample justice, giving anger free rein and committing great sin.

(Teaching, Practice, Faith, Enlightenment)

Yet he also said this, rejoicing: "Had my great teacher Honen not been sent away by authorities, how should I have gone into exile? Had I not gone into exile, how could I have hoped to convert the people of Echigo, who live in such a remote place? All this is owing to my teacher."[75] There was not a trace of poignancy in his words.

[75] From *The Biography.*

After five years of harsh exile, Shinran moved east to the Kanto area to continue preaching and teaching. One day the mountain monk Bennen, who had sworn to kill Shinran, appeared before him in broad daylight with drawn sword. Shinran "strode out to meet Bennen, swerving neither right nor left,"[76] then treated him as a friend and equal, gently assuring him that were he in Bennen's place, he too would have set out to kill Shinran, and adding that killing and being killed were alike opportunities to spread the teachings of Buddha. This encounter with Shinran's great and compassionate faith had a transforming impact on Bennen, who went on to become Myohobo, a disciple of Buddha and Shinran's devoted attendant.

[76] From *The Biography.*

Another time, while Shinran was preaching door-to-door, he was denied shelter in a snowstorm by a man named Hino Zaemon, who had contempt for Buddhism. Shinran calmly slept in the snow with a stone for pillow, and as a result Hino Zaemon, too, found salvation and became his disciple. Such episodes can well be said to exemplify "Pure Land compassion" in practice.

Shinran's greatest trial came when for the sake of the salvation of untold billions he disowned Zenran, his firstborn child. On the twenty-ninth day of the fifth month of 1256, at the age of eighty-four, Shinran sent a letter to his fifty-year-old son ending their relationship. Zenran was a heretic who not only claimed that his father had given him secret teachings in the middle of the night but also prayed to the old gods of Shinto, told fortunes, and otherwise desecrated the true teachings; realizing this, Shinran could not look the other way. When Zenran remained deaf to repeated admonishments, Shinran made the agonized decision to sever all ties with him, writing:

> My grief knows no words, but from this day forth I am no longer your parent, nor do I recognize you as my son. Nothing could sadden me more.

(Letter of Disownment)

This action brought harsh criticism, as people wondered what kind of Buddhist teaching breaks up families and scoffed that anyone unable to lead his own son to salvation could hardly hope to save others. It was perhaps inevitable that on top of suspicion, censure, and persecution, Shinran would suffer name-calling and derision. But had he overlooked Zenran's behavior out of misguided parental affection and rejoiced alone in his own salvation, resolving to do something about his son's salvation only after going to the Pure Land, what then? Untold billions, from the time of Shinran on into the limitless future, would have missed out on salvation.

With tears of gratitude at his unpayable debt to Amida, on his deathbed Shinran made this statement:

> My life at an end, I go to the Pure Land. But like the waves off Wakanoura Bay that endlessly come and go, I will return. When one person is happy, know that there are two. When two are happy, know that there are three. One will be me, Shinran.

(Last Words)

Till the very end, Shinran devoted his life to the salvation of mankind. Yet he always reflected with painful awareness that as he himself lacked even a smattering of true compassion, to think of saving others would be presumptuous. The true work of leading others to salvation could come only after he had achieved the enlightenment of a buddha. Indeed, he will always continue to return among us, like the ceaseless waves of the sea. Whether happy or sad, we are never alone. Shinran is always with us.

To review, when Shinran, in speaking of "Pure Land compassion," refers to "quickly attaining buddhahood," he is encouraging us to quickly *gain assurance of* attaining buddhahood: let this never be forgotten.

Close Translation of
Section V of *Tannisho*

I, Shinran, have never once said the nembutsu for the repose of my mother or father.

This is because all sentient beings, without exception, have in the course of various lives and states of existence been parent and sibling to me. In the next life I must attain buddhahood and save each one.

Were the nembutsu a good act that we did through our own power, we might direct the benefit of the nembutsu toward our parents and so save them; instead we must only abandon self-power and quickly attain the enlightenment of a buddha in the Pure Land. Then we can use transcendent powers and expedient means to save first those with whom we share deep bonds, whatever karmic suffering they may have sunk to in the six realms through the four modes of birth.

These were his words.

11

Funerals and Memorial Services
Are Not for the Dead

I, Shinran, have never once said the nembutsu for the repose of my mother or father.

(Tannisho, Section V)*

The idea that funerals and memorial services bring peace to the departed is firmly entrenched in many people's minds.

In ancient India, one of Śākyamuni's disciples inquired, "Is it true that if we recite edifying scriptures around the dead, they will be born in a good place?" The Buddha silently picked up a stone and tossed it into a pond. As it sank, he pointed to the spot and asked in return, "If you walked around the pond chanting 'Stone, rise! Stone, rise!' do you think the stone would float up to the surface?"

The stone sank of its own weight. Mere words could never cause it to rise. In the same way, instructed the Buddha, people's fate after death is determined by their own actions (karmic power).[77] It is impossible for any kind of sutra reading to change the fortunes of the departed.

[77] See also Glossary, "law of karma."

The idea that sutra-reading could bring about the salvation of the dead was not originally part of Buddhism. The teachings of the Buddha throughout his lifetime of eighty years were always for the living, falling like rain on the hearts and minds of the suffering. It is said that he never carried out any funerals or services for the dead. From the start, Buddhism eschewed such worldly, formalistic rituals and offered instruction rather about true emancipation—turning away from ignorance and achieving enlightenment. Yet today, many self-styled Buddhists take it for granted that rituals of funerals, services, and sutra readings do benefit the dead. Some superstitions die hard.

In the midst of such turmoil, the confession at the top of this chapter resounds like thunder from the blue: "I, Shinran, have never once said the nembutsu for the repose of my mother or father." "Repose" refers to requiem services, which are carried out in the belief that they will ensure the happiness of the dead. Shinran lost his father at the age of four and his mother at the age of eight; what must have been his grief when he thought of them? Surely the image of his dead parents haunted him above all else. Even so, he denies ever having said a single nembutsu on their behalf. Of course, this statement refers not only to the act of saying the nembutsu, but to all Buddhist services carried out with the intent of ensuring the happiness of the dead. It may thus be rephrased: "I, Shinran, have never once said the nembutsu, read a sutra, or held a memorial service to please my dead parents."

Shocking, you may think. To priests who calmly urge services for the repose of ancestors' souls, on the pretext that the dead appreciate nothing more than having sutras read on their behalf, and to lay people who accept this is a given, Shinran's pronouncement is baffling. To many people it may sound cold and callous. But with this sensational confession, Shinran, who revered his parents more than anyone, shattered the common people's deeprooted illusion and showed them the true way to honor their dead.

The monk Kakunyo (1270–1351), Shinran's descendant, lamented the existence of monks who made funerary and memorial rites their main job, ignoring the fact that Shinran never performed them. Let us quote Kakunyo's words:

> Shinran used to say, "When I die, cast my body into the River Kamo and feed it to the fishes." This was because he wanted to impress on people that they should care little for the body and make faith their top priority. Therefore it is wrong to make much of funerals. They should be stopped. *(Notes Rectifying Heresy)*

Why did Shinran make this shocking declaration? He did it to instruct people that rather than worry about the disposition of remains, which are like the empty shell of a locust, they should hurry above all to resolve the fate of the eternal self (acquire other-power faith). Therefore, concludes Kakunyo, rather than give importance to funerals, it would be better to call a halt to them.

Kakunyo disinherited his son, Zonkaku, for violating this teaching of Shinran's. In his *Record of Memorials* and elsewhere,

Zonkaku actually wrote such things as this: "After your parents die, you should strive to repay the debt you owe them, taking special care to carry out Buddhist services for the repose of their souls." "The best way to memorialize your parents is to say the nembutsu on their behalf." Such ideas are clearly subversive to Shinran's teaching that the practice of seeking the repose of the dead should be entirely done away with, and so it is fitting that Zonkaku was disowned.

The Buddhist world today is clearly violating Shinran's teaching, just as Zonkaku did, and is in that sense suffering from a sickness unto death. Without prompt reflection on the golden words of Shinran, Buddhism will become an empty shell.

Then are funerals, memorial services, and gravesite visits meaningless? No. To those who have heard Buddhist truth they are occasions for thanksgiving and rejoicing in Amida's salvation, and to those in ignorance of the truth they are chances to form bonds with Amida, the Buddha of Infinite Life.

Year in and year out, we read of significant traffic deaths. Told that many thousands of people died in accidents the previous year, we register no surprise but only stare aimlessly at the statistics, numb to the reality of death. Our desires keep us in a whirlwind of activity from morning to night, with no time to sit and contemplate the self. In the midst of such busyness, attending a funeral or kneeling at a grave can provide a precious chance to take a hard look at one's life: "I too must one day die. Am I not idling my life away?"

Being forced to face the cold fact of one's mortality is sobering. It is our hope that funerals and memorial services will be not empty rituals but occasions to deeply consider the crucial question of one's ultimate fate—eternal suffering or eternal bliss—and seek liberation: the acquisition of other-power faith.

Close Translation of
Section VI of *Tannisho*

That those who solely recite the nembutsu apparently argue about "my disciples" and "other people's disciples" is an outrage.

I, Shinran, do not have even a single disciple.

This is why: if by my own designs I brought people to say the nembutsu, they might be my disciples, but since they do so solely through the working of Amida, for me to call them "my disciples" would indeed be deplorable.

We come together when conditions bring us together, and part when conditions separate us. It is unreasonable for people to say that "anyone who turns his back on his teacher and says the nembutsu with another will not attain birth in the Pure Land." Do they mean to take back the faith bestowed by Amida, as if it belonged to them? Such a claim is preposterous.

When we come into accord with the truth of other-power we know gratitude to Buddha, and gratitude to our teachers as well.

These were his words.

12

No Disciples:
Shinran's Love for One and All

I, Shinran, do not have even a single disciple.   (*Tannisho*, Section VI)

Many Buddhist temple priests regard their parishioners as possessions and fear their departure as a diminishing of assets. For temples that rely on funerals and memorial services as a source of revenue, prosperity hinges on the number of parishioners. The fewer the parishioners, naturally, the greater the burden shouldered by each family. Patrons become disgruntled, wondering why, if offerings are a matter of free will, their donation to cover temple expenses has to be so high. They soon depart, switching to a religion that promises worldly benefits such as higher income, better health, and safety.

The masses are struggling in the welter of life's distress. Caught in the swirling waters of blind passions, they are searching for a lifeline. Instead of being exhorted not to drink the muddy water, they need to be rescued and given clear water to drink; but because the temples do not preach liberation from suffering, young men and women keep their distance and merely laugh at the notion of paying ritual visits to a temple.

As the steep decline in worshippers leaves temples everywhere in dire straits, priests lay aside their duties and go into business until one can hardly tell which is their main occupation. Wearing two hats is not enough to alleviate financial distress, however, so they resort to scrambling for parishioners and currying favor. When a renowned Buddhist preacher comes to the area, they go into a dither. Fearful lest their parishioners desert them, they go on the attack, spreading calumny about the interloper and conniving to drive him away.

The advice column of one national newspaper in Japan contained a letter from a woman in her fifties, troubled because the head priest of her temple had told her that her late mother was "pitiable," implicitly pressuring her to hold a memorial service. Such tactics, which may strike one as either offensive bullying or the desperate shrieks of temples hemorrhaging supporters, are all too common.

Wrongheaded clergy such as these are called to serious reflection by Shinran's words: "I do not have even a single disciple."

Of course, that Shinran had many disciples is a matter of historical record. We know from various historical documents, including a registry of the names of his disciples, that between sixty and seventy people studied under him in intimate association. Then why claim to have no disciples? The statement rises out of a deep self-awareness.

Shinran never looked on these people or anyone as his disciples. He was incapable of entertaining such a thought. On the surface it may indeed appear that he opened others' eyes to the crucial question of their fate for eternity, got them to listen earnestly to Buddhist teaching, and so saved them; but Shinran knew differently, better than anyone else.

> I do not know good from evil
> or right from wrong.
> I lack the slightest mercy or compassion,
> yet out of a desire for honor and wealth, I want to lead others.

(Hymns of Compunction)

Although he is totally ignorant and unqualified to stand above others, says Shinran, in his lust for recognition and riches he craves being kowtowed to as teacher; he is depraved and despicable. This is the heartfelt confession of one to whom it has been clearly revealed that he is trapped within the desire for fame and fortune.

> Lacking the slightest mercy or compassion,
> I cannot presume to benefit others.
> If not for the ship of Amida's Vow,
> how should anyone cross the sea of tribulation?

(Hymns of Lament and Reflection)

Shinran makes it clear that he has not a mite of mercy or compassion, and so could never lead anyone to salvation; the salvation of humanity is possible only due to Amida's great compassion. This is the anguished confession of one who sees clearly both his own evil, hypocritical nature and the Primal Vow that never judges, never forsakes.

> The painful sea of birth and death knows no bounds.
> Long have we been sinking in its waters.
> Only the ship of Amida's universal Vow
> will take us aboard and carry us across without fail.

(Hymns on the Masters)

Had his followers listened to Buddhism and been saved—gained certainty of birth in the land of infinite light[78]—due to Shinran's efforts, then they could be called his disciples. But since all is the doing of Amida's great compassion, declares Shinran, for him to call anyone his disciple is out of the question.

Dipping into the stream, Shinran knew its source. He understood clearly that having his eyes opened to the question of his ultimate fate, listening with an impassioned spirit to Buddhism, and receiving true happiness in this life were all due to the great workings of Amida Buddha. He knew that through profound bonds we are all born into this world as human beings, we are all alike nurtured by Amida and enjoy walking in his supreme Way, and we are all brothers and sisters with no distinctions of high and low. Therefore Shinran reaches out to the whole human race as family and fellow travelers.

In an age of rigid class divisions, Shinran manifested burning love for all mankind, inviting one and all to join him in the supreme Way with these words: "I, Shinran, do not have even a single disciple."

[78] The land of infinite light: The Pure Land.

Close Translation of
Section VII of *Tannisho*

He of the nembutsu is on the path of no hindrance. Why is this so? Before the one who has true faith, gods of heaven and earth bow down in reverence, and evil spirits and false teachings can pose no obstacle. Such a one is unaffected by any recompense for evil, and beyond the reach of every possible good; thus he is on the path of no hindrance.

These were his words.

13

What Happens
When We Are Saved by Amida?

He of the nembutsu is on the path of no hindrance.   (*Tannisho*, Section VII)

This famous line from the opening of Section VII has been the subject of much commentary. The "path of no hindrance" is variously interpreted as the "absolute path where no impediment exists" or the "one and only passageway where nothing forms a barrier," but few people really understand what it is all about.

Two sentences later we read, "Such a one is unaffected by any recompense for evil, and beyond the reach of every possible good." Some readers actually take this to mean that those who say the nembutsu are free of feelings of guilt, or will escape any negative outcomes of their wrongdoing. This is a misinterpretation of the "path of no hindrance."

To grasp the concept correctly, we must begin by affirming that the ultimate goal of Buddhism is birth in the Pure Land. Therefore, the hindrance spoken of here means anything that will prevent, or interfere with, such birth. Once we are saved by Amida, whatever evil we commit for whatever reason cannot possibly affect the diamond faith[79] of absolute certainty of birth in the Pure Land. This is why *Tannisho* asserts that "such a one is unaffected by any recompense for evil" and avows that "he of the nembutsu is on the path of no hindrance."

Why is it that even if we commit evil, our birth in the Pure Land is unhindered? Section I of *Tannisho* says this:

> Nor is there any need to fear evil, since no evil can block the working of Amida's Primal Vow.

[79] Diamond faith: Faith that is impervious to any attack.

Once we have encountered Amida's salvation, whatever sin we may commit, there is no fear that our sinfulness will keep us from birth in the Pure Land. Those saved by Amida's Vow are filled with a settled conviction that birth in the Pure Land is certain—a conviction that no evil can shake. It is because nothing can destroy or interfere with the world of other-power faith, a world beyond description, beyond explanation, and beyond understanding, that Shinran proclaims it the "path of no hindrance."

At the same time, no practice, however diligently carried out, can yield any outcome comparable to the wonder of this world, which is of all recompenses "supreme in the universe of ten directions," or greatest in the cosmos. This is why *Tannisho* declares the world of other-power faith "beyond the reach of every possible good" and proclaims that "there can be no greater good than the nembutsu" (Section I).

Then who is "he of the nembutsu"? The expression might appear to include any and all who intone "Namu Amida Butsu," but this is not so. Just as tears, though scientifically the same, may represent sadness or frustration or joy, the nembutsu may be spoken in many different states of mind. For example, the words could be uttered as a lucky charm when passing a graveyard at night, as an expression of grief on the passing of a loved one, or as a line of dialogue in a play.

Some see saying the nembutsu as first among various good acts ("foremost of myriad good acts"). To others it represents far and away the greatest good ("exceeding myriad good acts") and so they devote themselves to it exclusively. Shinran, who laid primary importance on the heart of the one saying the nembutsu, lumped these together as "people of self-power nembutsu." He distinguished them from those who are so full of happiness at their salvation that they cannot help saying the nembutsu in an outpouring of joy. These he called "people of other-power nembutsu"— that is, people who say the nembutsu through the power of Amida's Vow.

Shinran's "he of the nembutsu" always refers to the latter, one who has been saved by Amida and so attained other-power faith. This is made clear in the following sentence, where he rephrases it as "the one who has true faith." Once we gain other-power faith, nothing can stand in the way of our birth in the Pure Land. This is why Shinran proclaimed that "He of the nembutsu is on the path of no hindrance."

Close Translation of
Section VIII of *Tannisho*

The nembutsu is, for the one who has true faith, not a practice or an act of goodness. Because it is not performed through the designs of the self, it is not a practice. Because it is not a good done through the designs of the self, it is not an act of goodness. It is wholly other-power and free of self-power, and so for the one of true faith it is not a practice or an act of goodness.

These were his words.

14

The Great Faith and the Great Practice

The nembutsu is, for the one who has true faith, not a practice or an act of goodness.

(*Tannisho*, Section VIII)

Section I of *Tannisho* affirms that "there can be no greater good than the nembutsu," and Section II that there is no path to birth in Paradise other than the nembutsu. The reader might well assume that because the nembutsu is the greatest good of all, it should be said ("practiced") as often as possible. Yet here in Section VIII we read the surprising news that *for the one who has true faith* the nembutsu is not an act of goodness or a practice to devote oneself to. What can Shinran mean by this? The answer lies only in a correct understanding of the phrase "one who has true faith."

"One who has true faith" means "one who is saved by Amida." The nembutsu said by the saved is "other-power nembutsu," where the one saying the nembutsu is brought to do so completely through Amida's intense desire. The nembutsu said by those not saved by Amida is "self-power nembutsu," where the one saying it does so to keep from going to hell, hoping that Amida will save him for his diligence in repeating "Namu Amida Butsu." Such people see the nembutsu as a practice or good act to be performed for the purpose of salvation.

With other-power nembutsu, all such self-power judgment is annihilated and the individual is brought to say the nembutsu through Amida's powerful Vow. Other-power nembutsu is "not a practice or an act of goodness" that the devotee undertakes on his own, out of prudence or discretion. Rather, it is a practice and a good act that is bestowed on the devotee by Amida Buddha, and so it is also known as the Great Practice.

Shinran elaborates on this as follows:

> The Great Practice is to utter the Name of the Buddha of Unimpeded Light.[80] This practice encompasses all good deeds and contains all sources of merit.[81] It is a treasure-filled ocean of merit, the only truth, that fills the practitioner to overflowing with exceeding swiftness. Hence it is called the Great Practice.

To paraphrase: The Great Practice is to say the Name of Amida Buddha, "Namu Amida Butsu," which contains all good acts and all sources of merit. In the instant of belief[82] the Name becomes one[83] with the devotee, filling him or her with great goodness and merit; it is a vast ocean of treasure, the one and only absolute source of goodness and merit. This is why becoming one with the Name and saying it is called the Great Practice.

Let us review some central points from *Tannisho*. Section I declares that for Amida's salvation, "the sole requirement is faith." In Section VI, this faith is stated to be "faith bestowed by Amida"—that is, other-power faith. We are instructed in the same section that reciting the nembutsu on receiving faith is something we do only through Amida's strong desire: we say the nembutsu "solely through the working of Amida." The faith and the nembutsu that we receive from Amida are truly the Great Faith and the Great Practice.

The great virtue of Namu Amida Butsu enters through the ears and achieves oneness with us, spreads through our entire being and pours out through the mouth, flowing back into the great treasure-filled ocean of Namu Amida Butsu.

Feelings, whether of happiness or loneliness, are neither support nor hindrance. Going further, the believer does not rely on belief, and the practitioner does not rely on practice. Faith and practice that are granted by Amida Buddha become one with the incomprehensible sea of the Vow. The heart that believes and the heart that chants the nembutsu are alike the working of Namu Amida Butsu alone. That power is what moves the believer; the one of true faith is subject to that power. This is why the teachings of Shinran are called "absolute other-power."

(Teaching, Practice, Faith, Enlightenment)

[80] The Buddha of Unimpeded Light: Amida Buddha.

[81] Merit: Happiness and that which works to bring about happiness.

[82] The split second when all doubt in Amida's Vow is eradicated.

[83] Inseparably one, like fire and charcoal in a live coal.

Close Translation of
Section IX of *Tannisho*

"Even though I say the nembutsu, no desire to dance with joy arises within me, and neither do I wish to hasten to the Pure Land. What could be the meaning of this?"

I asked the master this, and he replied, "I have wondered that very thing. And the same thought has come to you! When I consider carefully, it is precisely my inability to rejoice over what should make me dance with joy in the sky and on earth that shows my birth in the Pure Land is truly settled.

"What suppresses our joy and prevents us from rejoicing is the working of the blind passions. And yet Buddha knew this beforehand and called us 'foolish beings made of blind passions.' Thus, knowing that the compassionate Vow of other-power is for us, who are such beings, we find it all the more trustworthy.

"It is also the working of the blind passions that makes us have no thought of hastening to the Pure Land, and causes us to wonder forlornly if we will die when we are even slightly ill. This old home of suffering where for countless kalpas we have transmigrated is hard for us to leave; and the Pure Land of bliss, where we have yet to be born, arouses no longing in us. Indeed, how powerful are our blind passions!

"But reluctant though we are to leave, when our ties to this world run out and our strength fails at the end, we will go to that land. Amida takes special pity on those who have no desire to go there quickly. Knowing this, we find his Vow of great compassion all the more trustworthy, and realize that our birth in the Pure Land is settled.

"If we had hearts of leaping, dancing joy and wished to go quickly to the Pure Land, we might wonder whether we had any blind passions."

These were his words.

15

"No Desire to Dance in Joy": Shinran's Lack of Joy Is Only Half the Story

"Even though I say the nembutsu, no desire to dance with joy arises within me, and neither do I wish to hasten to the Pure Land. What could be the meaning of this?" I asked the master this, and he replied, "I have wondered that very thing. And the same thought has come to you!"

(*Tannisho*, Section IX)

Some people say outright that it's no wonder they feel no joy, since Shinran said he had no joy in his heart, either. They even go so far as to declare that rejoicing is wrong. Here we see another peril of reading *Tannisho*.

This section records a conversation between Shinran and Yuien that is prone to distortion for the very reason that the statements in it are so easy to identify with. It contains turns of phrase that allow people to sympathize with Shinran and conveniently justify the lack of penitence and joy in their own faith on grounds that the inability to rejoice is only natural.

Yuien confessed, "I say the nembutsu, yet I feel no joy that makes me want to get up and dance. I feel no desire to go quickly to the Pure Land, either. How could this be?" Shinran's reply to this frank unburdening is straightforward: "I have asked myself that very question. The same thought has come to you, has it!"

Shinran's admission is the penitence of one who is saved by Amida; it has nothing whatever to do with the discontent of phony believers who, lacking penitence and joy, pride themselves on their joyless state. He continues:

"Even though our ties are cut to the worlds of suffering where we have wandered for innumerable lifetimes, and we are saved into a vast realm, we feel no joy; we are perfidious and utterly beyond salvation. Isn't it true, Yuien? What a comfort it is to know that even as I am, I am Amida's only child!"

Recovery from serious physical illness brings happiness. How much greater must be the joy of someone who, lacking hope of salvation at any time, from the limitless past and on into the future, is filled to overflowing with happiness that is "unnamable, inexplicable, inconceivable," as he is brought level with Miroku[84] and made the virtual equal of all the buddhas in the universe! Naturally such a person should feel like dancing for joy in heaven and on earth.

What prevents this is the worldly passions that blind us with desire and attachment. Maddened with these passions, utterly ungrateful, the one who is saved can do nothing but feel contrition for his evil nature. Shinran put it this way in *Teaching, Practice, Faith, Enlightenment*:

> How grievous! As I, most foolish Shinran, am swallowed in the vast sea of lust and troubled by the great mountain of [desire for] fame and wealth, I neither rejoice in having become one of the truly settled[85] nor take pleasure in nearing the realization of Buddha's enlightenment. How shameful! How sad!

Some have criticized these sentiments as self-tormenting, but surely they come from the heart. Yet behind this contrition lies joy, as we can see in this quote from later in Section IX:

> And yet Buddha knew this beforehand and called us "foolish beings made of blind passions." Thus, knowing that the compassionate Vow of other-power is for us, who are such beings, we find it all the more trustworthy.

In the distant past, Amida Buddha made his Vow in full knowledge that every human being is nothing but a mass of blind passions. What can we do but feel profound gratitude? Again in the epilogue to *Tannisho*, Shinran's joy rings out:

> Pondering the Vow of Amida, which rose from five kalpas of contemplation, I realize it was entirely for me, Shinran alone. I am profoundly grateful for the Primal Vow through which Amida resolved to save me, laden as I am with unfathomable evil karma.

Through untold aeons of deep deliberation, Amida worked out the Primal Vow. Its meaning is brought home to me through

[84] Miroku, "the Buddha of the future," is at the highest spiritual stage but one, just short of buddhahood.

[85] The truly settled: Those who have been saved in this life by Amida into absolute happiness, becoming assured of attaining buddhahood whenever life comes to an end.

reflection, and I see that it was all for my sake alone. How thankful I am for the Primal Vow, which Amida bestirred himself to make for my salvation, burdened as I am with evil and sin beyond reckoning!

It is precisely because he knew this profound joy that Shinran said contritely, in full awareness of his blind obstinacy, "I have wondered that very thing. And the same thought has come to you!"

People who have never crossed the threshold of Buddhism may take a narrow perspective—they may "look at the sky through the eye of a needle," as the proverb goes—and defiantly maintain that joylessness is only to be expected, but Shinran's admission belongs in a completely different dimension. Those who have not encountered Amida's salvation are naturally impenitent and joyless; how could it be otherwise?

The worldly passions also explain why we have no desire to hasten to the Pure Land, and why when we suffer any physical ailment we wonder forlornly if we will die. Although we live in a realm of continual suffering, where we have been transmigrating since ages past until now, that realm has become as dear to us as an old home; we feel no longing for the Pure Land of peace, nor any desire to go there quickly. This is our true nature.

The blind passions rage like a storm. Seeing their effects fills one with renewed assurance that Amida's Vow was for oneself alone, bringing home with even greater force the certainty of birth in the Pure Land. That is the meaning of Shinran's declaration, "Knowing this, we find his Vow of great compassion all the more trustworthy, and realize that our birth in the Pure Land is settled." The more we come to see our inherent self as it really is—numb, unable to rejoice when it should—the more compelled we are to exult in the wonder of salvation.

Shinran explained it using this analogy:

> Hindrances of sin become the substance of merit.
> It is just as with ice and water:
> The greater the ice, the greater the water.
> The greater the hindrance, the greater the virtue.

(Hymns on the Masters)

Amida's salvation melts the recalcitrant ice of blind passions ("sin") into the water of the joy of salvation ("virtue"). The greater the ice, the greater the water; thus the very Shinran who is the vilest and most depraved of sinners is indeed the happiest, most blessed being alive.

In this analogy, ice is the heart that should rejoice but cannot (*bonno*, or blind passions), and water is the joy (*bodai*) of feeling "his Vow of great compassion [to be] all the more trustworthy," and of knowing "that our birth in the Pure Land is settled." The wonder of having one's inexhaustible blind passions brought to light and transformed into limitless contrition and happiness is contained in the Buddhist phrases *bonno soku bodai* ("passion turns to virtue") and *ten'aku jozen* ("evil turns to good").

The more clearly Shinran sees his lack of a joyful mind, the more deeply he rejoices in his salvation. This is the great sea of faith—the world of faith that is granted by Amida Buddha, a world where mind and words fail: "It is only inconceivable, unnamable, inexplicable faith." Shinran is filled to overflowing with praise and devotion.

(Teaching, Practice, Faith, Enlightenment)

Close Translation of
Section X of *Tannisho*

The concept of the nembutsu is no-concept, for it is unnamable, inex-
plicable, inconceivable. So said the master.

16

What Is "Namu Amida Butsu"?

The concept of the nembutsu is no-concept, for it is unnamable, inexplicable, inconceivable. So said the master.

(Tannisho, Section X)

The word "nembutsu" appears so often in *Tannisho* that many people are under the impression that they need only say the nembutsu and they will be saved—but that is a mistake. Section I, in which the entire book is encapsulated, states plainly that "the sole requirement is faith." Therefore, all subsequent mention of the nembutsu needs to be understood as applying to those who have already gained faith.

As we have seen, Shinran refers to the nembutsu spoken by those who are saved by Amida—those who have gained faith—as "other-power nembutsu." The nembutsu described here in Section X as "the concept of no-concept," too, is clearly other-power nembutsu.

Differing interpretations of this opening phrase have been offered by various commentators. These include: "the correct understanding of the nembutsu is that it cannot be understood"; "the purpose of no purpose"; "the logic of no logic"; "the intention of Buddha to free humanity from distorted thinking." In fact, the word here translated as "concept" means human calculation—all our doubts, deliberations, imaginings, and knowledge having to do with Amida's Vow.

"I say the nembutsu gratefully and live a life filled with gratitude, so surely nothing bad will happen to me."

"I say the nembutsu so much that surely I won't go to a bad place when I die."

"I believe in Amida, so I'll be all right when I die."

"I can't help myself in this life, but when I die, surely Amida will save me."

"Saying the nembutsu doesn't move me. I wonder if everything is all right."

"My heart is wicked, but Amida knows all about it, so I needn't worry."

"I wonder if it's true that just saying the nembutsu is enough?"

There is no end to such examples, all of which are the expression of the mind that doubts Amida's Vow. Such calculation derives from the mind of self-power. So long as this self-power mind exists, we cannot possibly encounter Amida's salvation or enter into the realm of other-power.

Shinran instructs us, "Abandon self-power. The intention to do so is also self-power, so abandon that as well." His teaching holds firm on this point. He insists that we abandon self-power and enter other-power.

"No-concept" is the state in which all trace of the mind of self-power has vanished or been purged. This is why Shinran said that "the concept of the nembutsu is no-concept" and that other-power nembutsu, being the nembutsu of a mind purged of self-power (imaginings and deliberations about Amida's Vow) is "unnamable, inexplicable, inconceivable."

Amida Buddha created "Namu Amida Butsu" to realize his Vow to save all beings into absolute happiness. Namu Amida Butsu is known as "the Name." To understand the need for the Name, let us use an analogy from the medical world. The mere existence of principles for curing illness cannot save patients' lives. The principles must be discovered, and a physician must prepare medicine based on them. "Namu Amida Butsu" can be thought of as a physic (miracle drug) created by the physician Amida Buddha, the expression of his compassionate desire to take away the suffering of the human race and give lasting happiness to all. Each human mind is deeply defiled from untold ages past and lacking a grain of truth, unable to free itself from suffering. Taking pity on the human condition, stirred by a passionate desire to save humankind Amida spent unimaginably long aeons disciplining mind and body with utmost fervor. What emerged is the crystallization of all virtue (goodness) in the universe: the Name "Namu Amida Butsu."

In *Teaching, Practice, Faith, Enlightenment*, Shinran explains the origin of the Name as follows:

> The sea of all sentient beings, from time immemorial until this very day and hour, is polluted with evil and lacking in a mind of purity; it is false and deceitful, lacking in a mind of truth. The Tathagata[86] felt sorrow and compassion for the sea of beings in affliction, and while for unimaginable aeons on end he carried out bodhisattva practices, not for a moment or an instant was his practice in the three modes tainted or lacking in sincerity. With purity of mind he brought about the realization of the perfect, unhindered, inconceivable, unnamable, inexplicable supreme virtue.

[86] Tathagata is one who has attained buddhahood. Here the reference is to Amida Buddha.

To paraphrase: The human heart, from ages past till now, has been and is stained with wickedness and lacking in purity; it contains nothing but falsehoods and drivel, with not an ounce of truth. Amida Buddha was saddened and moved to pity by the suffering and affliction of all beings. In his desire to save them, for a mind-bendingly long time he maintained absolute purity of thought, speech, and action. With that pure and sincere mind he devoted himself with all his might to discipline, bringing about the perfect, supreme virtue that cannot be named or explained or imagined: Namu Amida Butsu.

Rennyo explained it in simple terms.

> "Namu Amida Butsu" is written with only six Chinese characters, so it seems unlikely to possess any great virtue. Yet the virtue that lies within this six-character Name is supreme and profound, without limit.

(*The Letters*, Fascicle 5, Letter 13)

The Name "Namu Amida Butsu" is so short and simple that no one would suspect it of having great power, yet it has the great faculty of conferring absolute happiness on us. The power of Namu Amida Butsu is as vast as the sky.

In a split second Amida Buddha bestows on us the Name "Namu Amida Butsu" so that we become one with it, a state known as "oneness with Buddha" (the mind of Amida Buddha and the mind of the believer form a single entity) or "complete acquisition of Buddha's wisdom" (receiving into oneself the full virtue of the universe).

Shinran expressed his direct experience of this state in a hymn:

> If anyone in this evil, corrupt world
> has faith in the Vow of Amida,
> unnamable, inexplicable, inconceivable
> blessing fills his being.

(Hymns on the Masters)

Anyone at all who believes in the Primal Vow of Amida (receives Namu Amida Butsu) brims over with happiness beyond speech or understanding. Shinran is saying that just such blessing fills his own being.

Fusion of the believer and Namu Amida Butsu—the Name whose virtue is unnamable, inexplicable, and inconceivable—is faith that is unnamable, inexplicable, and inconceivable. No wonder Shinran said that the nembutsu that pours from the believer's lips is itself unnamable, inexplicable, and inconceivable!

The nembutsu is Amida Buddha's wisdom, which beggars human understanding. This is why Shinran said, "The concept of the nembutsu is no-concept."

Close Translation of
the Epilogue of *Tannisho*

All of the above assertions arise out of differences in faith. The late master related this story. In his day, Master Honen had many disciples, but few of the same faith as him; the discrepancy gave rise to a dispute between Shinran and his friends.

It came about this way. Shinran said, "My faith and the master's faith are the same." Some of the disciples, including Seikanbo and Nembutsubo, were appalled and argued the point: "How could your faith be the same as our master's faith?" Shinran replied, "The master's wisdom and learning are vast, and if I said mine were the same I would be wrong; but concerning faith that leads to birth there is no difference whatever. Our faith is the same."

The others persisted, "How can that possibly be?" As they were skeptical, in the end they decided to go before the master to have him arbitrate the matter. When they had presented the details, Honen said this: "My faith is the faith granted by Amida Buddha, and Shinran's faith is likewise the faith granted by Amida Buddha. Hence they are the same. Those who have different faith will surely not go to the Pure Land where I am going."

This account shows that even back then, those who believed only in Amida included some whose faith was not the same as Shinran's. Although I am repeating myself, I have set all this down in writing.

While the dewdrop of life clings precariously to this withered leaf of grass, I will go on listening to the misgivings of those who accompany me and tell them what the master said. I can only lament that after my eyes close for the final time there will be chaos. When people make the sort of claim written above and you are thrown into confusion, carefully read the sacred writings that accord with the late Master's thought and that he himself used.

The scriptures in general are a mix of the true and real with the provisional and expedient. That we abandon the provisional and take up the real, set aside the expedient and avail ourselves of the true, was the master's fundamental intent. Be absolutely sure not to misread the scriptures. I have excerpted several important passages and attached them to this book as a guide.

The master often said this:

> Pondering the Vow of Amida, which rose from five kalpas of contemplation, I realize it was entirely for me, Shinran, alone. I am profoundly grateful for the Primal Vow through which Amida resolved to save me, laden as I am with unfathomable evil karma.

Now as I reflect again on these heartfelt words of Shinran, they seem not a bit different from this wise saying of Shan-tao's:

> I am, now, a foolish being imbued with evil and caught in the cycle of birth and death, constantly submerged and constantly wandering for all these countless aeons, without ever a chance for liberation: this is clearly revealed to me.

I am humbly grateful for the words of Shinran in which he offers himself as an example in order to impress upon us that we are in delusion, unaware of the depths of our own evil and the vastness of Amida's benevolence.

Truly, we and others rarely speak of Amida's benevolence, addressing only matters of good and evil. But Shinran had this to say:

> Concerning good and evil alike I know nothing at all. If I knew thoroughly, as the Tathagata does, that an act was good, then I would know good, and if I knew with certainty, as the Tathagata does, that an act was evil, then I would know evil. In this world as fleeting and unstable as a burning house, inhabited by human beings beset by worldly passions, all is idleness and foolishness, utterly devoid of truth. Only the nembutsu is true.

Truly, I myself as well as others speak nothing but idle words. There is one painful fact, which is that when we debate among ourselves the nature of faith that leads one to say the nembutsu, or when we tell about it to others, in order to stop up others' mouths and end the discussion we claim that the master said things he never did. This is disgraceful and lamentable.

The words I have written are not my own, but as I have not explored all the sutras and commentaries, and as I lack familiarity with the depths of the scriptures, there are certain to be peculiarities. However, I have called to mind a mere fragment—a hundredth part—of our late Master Shinran's sayings and written it down here.

It would be very sad if anyone fortunate enough to say the nembutsu were not born directly into the Pure Land but instead had to dwell in a hinterland. So that there may be no difference in faith among fellow practitioners gathered in a single room, I have dipped my brush in ink and written this in tears.

I will call it *Tannisho* ["Lamenting the Deviations"]. It is not for everyone to see.

17

The Reality of Self-Power
and the Ocean of Other-Power Faith

Concerning good and evil alike I know nothing at all.   (*Tannisho*, Epilogue)

"I don't know the first thing about good and evil. It's beyond me."
A statement like this from Shinran makes us doubt our ears. Based
on this, some would even question his fitness to teach Buddhism.
But when you think about it, are our concepts of good and evil
really immutably valid?

Concepts of good and bad vary from one culture to another and
can shift over time within the same culture. In Japan, for example,
it's worse to be labeled a thief than a coward, but in the United
States "coward" bears a greater stigma. In Japan a punch is worse
punishment than a slap, but in the West a slap is more humiliating.
And in prewar Japan the slogan of the day was *umeyo fuyaseyo*
("bear children, swell the population!"), but nowadays anyone
with a large family receives expressions of sympathy. In fact, the
decline in Japan's birthrate has become so extreme that the govern-
ment and corporations are engaged in feverish efforts to support
young parents.

Over time, people and policies once hailed as good often fall
into disfavor. In the past, those who expanded their nation's terri-
tory were hailed as heroes, but today they are denigrated as
invaders. In feudal Japan, dying for one's lord or military ruler was
revered as an expression of *chu* or loyalty to one's superior, the
paramount samurai virtue, but from the late nineteenth century
on the term was used only in connection with dying for the
emperor, and nowadays many Japanese have never even heard of

it. Until the end of World War II, phrases like *shuken zaimin* ("sovereignty resides in the populace") and *roshi byodo* ("equality of labor and management") were taboo, seen as expressing dangerously democratic ideals, and anyone uttering them was liable to be thrown in prison as a subversive or a Communist. But in today's Japan, the emperor and the laborer are ostensibly equal. In some countries, a change of administration means a new constitution and general amnesty for prisoners, impeachment and conviction for yesterday's power holders. In this way, a nation's values are often turned on their head with the passage of time.

Even in the same place and time, opinions on right and wrong do not always coincide, but show great variation. The Japanese Supreme Court is composed of fifteen veteran justices whose verdicts are seldom if ever unanimous, more often coming down 10–5 or 7–8. The same phenomenon occurs in courts around the world. Justices each bring a unique perspective and set of impressions to their examination of the same briefs, and so disagree on whether the verdict should be guilty or not guilty—in essence, good or evil.

Saving lives, can cause suffering to others. The Great Hanshin Earthquake of 1995 was followed by a rash of suicides among the elderly—people rescued from the rubble of their collapsed homes only to lament later on that, having lost everything they cherished, they would rather have perished in the flames. Daring rescues, which took place on the unquestioned assumption that saving lives is always good, may exemplify good intentions gone astray.

Honesty is another cherished value but sometimes telling the truth can be brutal:

"Your baby looks like a monkey."

"Everyone will be relieved when you die."

"I only married you for your money."

Being entirely open can cause torment to others.

Shinran said, "I don't know the first thing about good and evil. It's beyond me." Rennyo, too, when asked why Shinran did a certain thing the way he did, replied this way:

I don't know either, but even concerning things we do not know you should bear in mind that we follow what Master Shinran has done.

(The Words of Rennyo Heard and Recorded During His Lifetime)

Our notions of good and evil are based on moral standards that
are in constant flux according to the time, place, and person. Yet
we make self-righteous, inflexible, arrogant protestations like these:

"My way of thinking is right."

"I at least know right from wrong."

"I refuse to believe what I cannot accept."

We take the same superior attitude even toward Amida Buddha's
Primal Vow. We will believe the Vow once we are satisfied that it
is good and right, we think, and not until then. Shinran chides
the foolishness of all our attempts to weigh Amida's unnamable,
inexplicable, inconceivable Primal Vow, in these words:

> No one, not even Miroku Bodhisattva, could fathom the
> wisdom of Buddha.

(Lamp for the Latter Age)

When not even the bodhisattva Miroku, who is one step away
from the enlightenment of a buddha, can comprehend or imagine
the wonders of Amida's Vow, how can ordinary, foolish humans
hope to understand Amida's peerless wisdom?

Once one is saved and embraced by Amida's unnamable, inexplicable, inconceivable Primal Vow, self-power—the mind that,
obsessed with good and evil, tries to fathom the Vow—is purged.
The believer is then neither desirous of good nor fearful of evil.
Shinran's admission that "Concerning good and evil alike I know
nothing at all" is none other than an expression of this great sea of
faith.[87]

[87] The world of other-
power faith received
from Amida Buddha.

18

The Universal Purpose of Life

In this world as fleeting and unstable as a burning house, inhabited by human beings beset by worldly passions, all is idleness and foolishness, utterly devoid of truth. Only the nembutsu is true.　　(*Tannisho*, Epilogue)

Shinran's statement above is sweeping. Truly, everything in this world is idle and foolish, without a particle of truth. *Tannisho* repeatedly offers statements that deny the value of all human enterprise—antisocial, anti-moral statements that violate common sense. But all reveal true faith.

Some nonreligious people are disgruntled by the word "faith," feeling that it has no connection to them. But we all have faith. Broadly speaking, "faith" does not apply only to belief in the supernatural. We have faith in our life, for example, believing we will live to see tomorrow, or in our health, believing we have years of healthy life ahead of us. Husbands and wives, parents and children have faith in one another. People place faith in wealth and possessions, or in honor and status. Marxists are people who believe in the ideal of a Communist society. What each of us believes in is up to us, but life is impossible without believing in *something*. Since living is believing, no one can be completely lacking in faith.

The betrayal of faith brings swift pain. Loss of health means physical suffering; a sweetheart's betrayal means the agony of a broken heart. Men and women crushed by the death of a spouse, parents anguished by the loss of a child, people whose wealth and good name lie in ashes—all alike exist in a dark vale of tears where the light of faith has gone out. The stronger our faith, the more we suffer and rage at its betrayal.

Our lives are a daily struggle, yet we were not born into this world to suffer. That is not why we live. Ultimately, the sole and universal purpose of our lives is to seek lasting joy and make it ours. Surely, then, we ought to look with the greatest of care into the genuineness of what it is we place our faith in. To what extent do we in fact ponder whether the things we trust are worthy of that trust or not?

Earthquakes, typhoon, lightning, fire, murder, injury, theft, illness, accidents, the deaths of loved ones, failure in business, layoffs: we live in a fragile world where anything may happen, any time. "The prosperous must decline," remind the magisterial opening lines of the medieval epic *The Tale of the Heike*. All at the summit of glory are heading for a fall. Likewise, the Buddhist saying "those who meet must part" reminds us that the joy of meeting is always followed by the sadness of farewell. Even if we overcome one trouble, we still live in an unsteady world where hopes and trust are endlessly betrayed. In vivid language, Shinran warns us that we inhabit a "world as fleeting and unstable as a burning house."

Though we may manage somehow to escape natural disasters and sickness, no one can escape the finality of death. What happens when we stand at death's door? Wealth and fame fade as swiftly as a flash of lightning. In the face of death, the greatest ruler is stripped of all authority, and no undying light meets the eye. To those who still persist in the delusion that what they believe in will last forever, Shinran's words resound like mighty thunder: "All is idleness and foolishness, utterly devoid of truth." There are no exceptions.

Time and again it has happened that a respected community leader, someone who counsels others on the dignity of life and exhorts people not to die but to live on with strength and courage, sends shock waves through society by suddenly hanging himself. The suicides of the famous, meanwhile, tend somehow to be glamorized. But unless the solemn purpose of life is understood, even debates over the right and wrong of suicide are themselves mere "idleness and foolishness."

Living in a world such as this is like dancing on a live volcano. The impulse to escape the anxiety of such an existence by choosing death is not incomprehensible. Against this background, Shinran's grand pronouncement stands out all the more:

"Only the nembutsu is true."

His voice calls to us: "Everyone! Gain the endless joy of life found in being firmly clasped, never to be abandoned, and say the nembutsu: there is no ultimate reason why you have been born as a human being but this."

Enormous effort and many tears went into the writing of *Tannisho*, solely to transmit this one message that Shinran preached throughout his ninety years of life.

Glossary

Amida; Amida Buddha: The Japanese pronunciation of the name of the buddha Amitābha [Infinite Light] or Amitāyus [Infinite Life]. (Throughout this book, we have opted to use the Japanese version of his name, rather than the Sanskrit.) Amida is supreme among the innumerable buddhas in the cosmos, all of whom achieved buddhahood through his power. *See also* Primal Vow.

birth *(ojo)*: Amida's salvation. Composed of characters meaning "to go" and "to be born." Shinran taught that the word has two meanings:
1) *futaishitsu ojo* (literally, "salvation without loss of the body"): being saved by Amida into absolute happiness in this life.
2) *taishitsu ojo* (literally, "salvation with loss of the body"): going to Amida's Pure Land at the moment of death and being reborn as a buddha.

blind passions; worldly passions *(bonno)*: Lust, anger, jealousy, and other delusions of the heart that trouble and torment us. Buddhism teaches that the human being is an aggregate of 108 blind passions; all humans are made of these passions, and nothing else.

bodhisattva: Seeker of true happiness; one who is striving to attain the enlightenment of a buddha.

buddha: One who has attained the highest level of enlightenment in the cosmos. Buddhism teaches that there are fifty-two levels of enlightenment, the highest of which is called the "enlightenment of a buddha." The only human being on this earth ever to achieve supreme enlightenment was Śākyamuni. Buddhism further teaches that the cosmos contains innumerable worlds similar to ours, with as many buddhas as there are grains of sand in the Ganges.

buddhahood: The enlightenment of a buddha. The highest of the fifty-two levels of enlightenment.

Buddhism of sages (*Shodo* **Buddhism):** Tendai, Shingon, Zen, and other forms of Buddhism in which devotees seek to attain enlightenment through ascetic practices.

cycle of birth and death; transmigration: Buddhism teaches that from ages past, each of us has been born and reborn countless times in a myriad of life forms. Just as a wheel keeps turning without end, so all beings travel endlessly back and forth among the various worlds of illusion, in constant suffering. Buddhism teaches that becoming free of this cycle is the ultimate purpose of human life.

expedient: Essential means of leading people to the truth.

false teachings; heresy: In the context of Buddhism, this means teachings that go against the law of karma. *See also* law of karma.

four modes of birth: The four possible ways that a sentient being may be born. These are: 1) birth from a womb; 2) birth from an egg; 3) birth from moisture; and 4) birth by sudden appearance. The phrase "four modes of birth" is used to refer to all sentient beings.

Honen (1133–1212): The founder of the Pure Land School of Buddhism *(Jodo Shu)*, and Shinran's teacher. Known for his profound learning and saintliness, he was widely revered as Japan's premier Buddhist scholar.

Hymn of True Faith (Shoshinge): A poem by Shinran in classical Chinese encapsulating his teachings on true faith.

Hymns on the Pure Land (Jodo wasan): Poems by Shinran in praise of Amida Buddha and his Pure Land.

Kakunyo (1270–1351): Shinran's descendant and a prominent master of True Pure Land Buddhism who faithfully transmitted the teachings of Shinran.

kalpa: Said to be a period of 432,000,000 years, "kalpa" is used to refer to an inconceivably long expanse of time.

Lamp for the Latter Age (Mattosho): A collection of Shinran's letters and sayings.

law of karma; law of cause and effect: The universal truth, woven through all Buddhist doctrine, that our good actions bring us good results (happiness), and, conversely, that our bad actions bring us bad results (unhappiness, disaster). This law dictates that everything that happens to us—good or bad—is determined by our own actions. These actions include actions of the mind (thoughts), actions of the mouth (speech), and actions of the body (behavior).

Letters, The (Gobunsho): A collection of letters written by Rennyo, consisting of eighty letters in five fascicles.

mind of self-power *(jiriki no kokoro)*: The human mind that seeks to resolve the crucial matter of the afterlife. It is the mind that endeavors to earn salvation through good deeds rather than through reliance solely on Amida. It refers to doubts or deliberations about Amida Buddha's Vow.

Mount Hiei: The site where Shinran practiced the Buddhism of the sages for twenty years. A mountain on the border between Kyoto and Shiga prefectures; site of the head temple of the Tendai sect of Buddhism.

Name *(myogo)*: The six-character "Namu Amida Butsu" (南無阿弥陀仏), which manifests Amida Buddha's vast compassion. Through the Name, Amida Buddha expressed his compassion in a form that human beings' finite minds can apprehend. It is the embodiment of truth that removes suffering for all people and grants eternal happiness.

nembutsu: Recitation of the words "Namu Amida Butsu."
    other-power —: The nembutsu that is spoken through the working of Amida Buddha. An expression of gratitude for the salvation granted by Amida. *See also* other-power.
    self-power —: The nembutsu that is spoken through one's own efforts. *See also* self-power.

Nichiren (1222–82): Founder of the Nichiren sect of Buddhism, which emphasizes the Lotus Sutra as the supreme scripture. Nichiren was a vocal opponent of Pure Land beliefs.

Nirvana: The Sanskrit term "Nirvana" literally means "extinguishment" (of worldly passions). In the context of True Pure Land Buddhism, it refers to the same level of enlightenment as Amida Buddha.

other-power *(tariki)*: The power of Amida Buddha (and nothing else). The working of his great compassion.

other-power faith *(tariki no shinjin)*: Completely unlike ordinary faith, the faith which Shinran taught is the gift of Amida Buddha, and so is called "other-power faith." It is also known as "twofold revelation" and "true faith." Shinran preached nothing but other-power faith. *See also* twofold revelation.

path of no hindrance *(muge no ichido)*: Absolute happiness. The state of mind of one who has been saved by Amida.

Primal Vow; Amida's Vow; the Vow *(hongan)*: Amida Buddha vowed to save all sentient beings into absolute happiness without fail.

Pure Land; Paradise *(jodo; gokuraku)*: The world of bliss inhabited by Amida Buddha, in which there is no suffering.

Pure Land Buddhism *(Jodo Shu)*: A school of Buddhism founded in Japan by Honen. Based on the Larger Sutra of Infinite Life, the Sutra of Contemplation on the Buddha of Infinite Life, and the Amida Sutra, it teaches salvation by Amida Buddha. After Honen's death, Pure Land Buddhism split into several sects.

Rennyo (1415–99): Shinran's descendant and a prominent master of True Pure Land Buddhism. Through his letters (collected as *Gobunsho* [The Letters]) and sermons, he transmitted Shinran's teachings faithfully to a vast number of people across Japan, bringing about a revival of this school. He wrote a warning to the reader at the end of *Tannisho* and also was responsible for placing the text under seal.

Śākyamuni (ca. 560–480 BC): The founder of Buddhism. He was born the son of a king in Nepal, but at the age of twenty-nine he left home in search of lasting happiness. He achieved supreme enlightenment at the age of thirty-five and became a buddha. From then until his death at age eighty, he preached the grace and compassion of Amida.

self-power *(jiriki)*: *See* mind of self-power.

sentient beings: *See* four modes of birth.

Shan-tao (613–81): A monk who was one of the most important figures in Pure Land Buddhism in China and who helped to develop Pure Land teachings.

Shinran (1173–1263): Founder of the True Pure Land school of Buddhism. A disciple of Honen. The first Buddhist monk to openly eat meat and marry, he taught true Buddhism through which all people—not just monks in mountaintop monasteries—can be saved. At age 35, banished from Kyoto in a clampdown by authorities, he declared himself "neither monk nor layman." His life was devoted to teaching about Amida's Vow. His main work is the monumental *Kyogyoshinsho* [Teaching, Practice, Faith, Enlightenment].

six realms of suffering: The realms of delusion through which sentient beings transmigrate. Specifically: hell (the world of extreme agony); the world of hungry ghosts (insatiable desire); the world of animals (the law of the jungle); the world of asuras (perpetual combat); the world of human beings (a mixture of pain and pleasure); and the world of celestial beings (ample pleasure that does not last).

sutras: Sermons delivered by Śākyamuni during the forty-five years between his attainment of Buddhist enlightenment at age thirty-five and his death at eighty, as recorded by his disciples.

***Teaching, Practice, Faith, Enlightenment (Kyogyoshinsho)*:** Shinran's magnum opus, which he carefully refined throughout his life.

True Pure Land Buddhism *(Jodo Shinshu)*: The teachings of Shinran, who learned the teachings of Pure Land Buddhism from Honen. Although Honen had over 380 disciples, few understood his teachings correctly, which is why after his death the school split into five sects. Shinran had no intention of setting up a new school of Buddhism, and established True Pure Land Buddhism solely to transmit his master's teachings faithfully. This sect thus contains no new teachings unique to Shinran, but continues the orthodox tradition of Pure Land Buddhism.

true settlement *(shojo)*: Salvation by Amida, in this life, to the fifty-first of the fifty-two stages of enlightenment. To become clearly settled in this life to attain buddhahood; absolute happiness.

twofold revelation: Faith that is beyond ordinary comprehension, in which the self that cannot be saved and the self that is saved are simultaneously and continuously revealed without a shadow of doubt.

Yuien (1222–89): One of the leading disciples of Shinran. Believed to be the author of *Tannisho*.

Bibliography

Shinran. *Hitanjukkai wasan* [Hymns of Lament and Reflection]. In *Shinshu shogyo zensho* [The Sacred Literatures of Shin Buddhism], Vol. 2. Edited by Shinshu Shogyo Zensho Hensanjo. Kyoto: Oyagi Kobundo, 1941. A collection of sixteen poems expressing sorrow over the author's own evil.

———. *Jodo wasan* [Hymns on the Pure Land]. In *Shinshu shogyo zensho*, Vol. 2. A collection of 188 poems in praise of Amida Buddha and his Pure Land.

———. *Koso wasan* [Hymns on the Masters]. In *Shinshu shogyo zensho*, Vol. 2. A collection of 119 poems in praise of the seven masters in India, China, and Japan who faithfully taught Amida's Vow, taking them up in historical order and introducing their contributions to Pure Land teachings.

———. *Kyogyoshinsho* [Teaching, Practice, Faith, Enlightenment]. In *Shinshu shogyo zensho*, Vol. 2. The author's master work, containing all of his teachings. After finishing a rough draft in his early fifties, Shinran continued to refine it for the rest of his life, editing and amending it.

———. *Mattosho* [Lamp for the Latter Age]. In *Shinshu shiryo shusei* [The Collected Texts of Shin Buddhism], Vol. 1. Edited by Mitsuyuki Ishida and Joryu Chiba. Kyoto: Dohosha, 1974. A collection of the letters and words of Shinran.

———. *Ondokusan* [Song of Amida's Grace and Virtue]. In *Shinshu shogyo zensho*, Vol. 2. A poem on the author's indebtedness to Amida and to the teachers who led him to salvation.

———. *Shoshinge* [Hymn of True Faith]. In *Shinshu shogyo zensho*, Vol. 2. A poem in classical Chinese encapsulating the author's teachings on salvation.

———. *Shozomatsu wasan* [Hymns on the Three Ages]. In *Shinshu shogyo zensho*, Vol. 2. A collection of poems teaching that Amida's Vow is the sole path to salvation.

———. *Yuishin sho mon'i* [Notes on "Essentials of Faith Alone"]. In *Shinshu shogyo zensho*, Vol. 2. A commentary on *"Essentials of Faith Alone"* by Seikaku.

———. *Zangi wasan* [Hymns of Compunction]. In *Shinshu shogyo zensho*, Vol. 2. A pair of poems at the end of the author's *Hymns on the Three Ages (Shozomatsu wasan)*.

Kakunyo. *Godensho* [The Biography]. In *Shinshu shogyo zensho*, Vol. 3. Edited by Shinshu Shogyo Zensho Hensanjo. Kyoto: Oyagi Kobundo, 1941. A life of Shinran written by his great-grandson.

———. *Gaijasho* [Notes Rectifying Heresy]. In *Shinshu shiryo shusei*, Vol. 1. A treatise correcting false doctrine and revealing the true teaching.

Rennyo. *Gobunsho* [The Letters]. In *Shinshu shiryo shusei*, Vol. 2. Edited by Osamu Katata. Kyoto: Dohosha, 1977. A collection of eighty letters in five fascicles. These lucid writings helped to disseminate Shinran's teachings throughout Japan.

Rennyo shonin goichidaiki kikigaki [The Words of Rennyo Heard and Recorded During His Lifetime]. In *Shinshu shogyo zensho*, Vol. 5. Edited by Shinshu Shogyo Zensho Hensanjo. Kyoto: Oyagi Kobundo, 1941. A record of the sayings, homilies, and deeds of Rennyo. Author unknown.

Map of Places That Appear in the Text

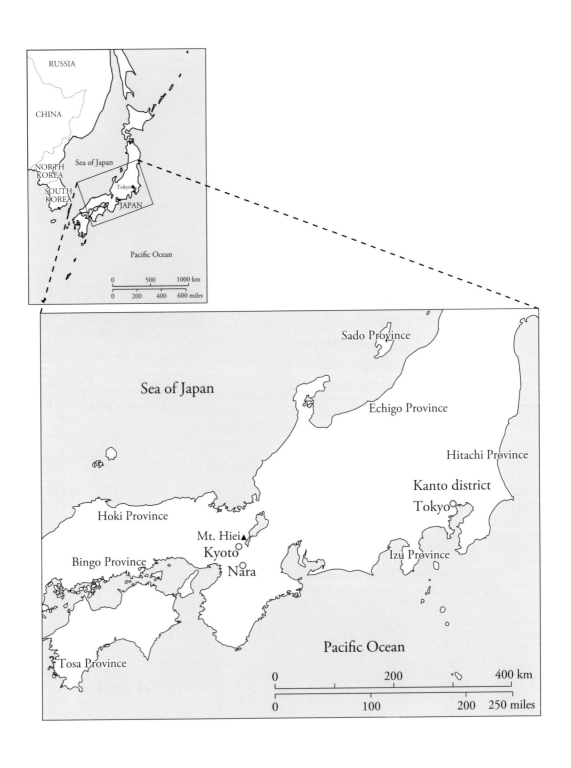

Timeline of the Development of Pure Land Buddhism

Japanese History	World History
942 **Genshin, author of *Essentials of Birth in the Pure Land*, is born in Nara.**	
1020 Murasaki Shikibu's *The Tale of Genji* appears and is one of the world's first known novels.	
1133 **Honen, founder of the Pure Land School of Buddhism, is born in the western region of Japan.**	
1173 Shinran is born in Kyoto.	
1175 **Honen founds the Pure Land School.**	
1180 Genpei War (–85).	
1181 Shinran enters the priesthood at Mount Hiei.	
1185 Establishment of the Kamakura Shogunate, the beginning of a two-tier power system shared between the emperor, with his imperial court, and samurai leaders.	
1201 Shinran encounters Honen and, through Amida's Vow, achieves the purpose of life. He then becomes Honen's disciple.	
1203 Shinran breaks with Buddhist monastic traditions of vegetarianism and celibacy by eating fish and taking a wife.	
	1204 The Siege of Constantinople in the Fourth Crusade and the decline of the Byzantine Empire.
1207 Exile of Honen and Shinran.	
	1215 King John of England seals the Magna Carta.

Japanese History	World History
1256 Shinran disowns Zenran, his first-born son.	
1263 Shinran dies in Kyoto.	
1271 **Kakunyo, author of *Notes Rectifying Heresy* and other important works, is born in Kyoto.**	
	1295 Marco Polo returns to Venice from his travels throughout Asia.
	1299 The Ottoman dynasty begins in the Middle East (–1922).
1415 **Rennyo, author of *The Letters*, is born in Kyoto.**	
	1453 The Fall of Constantinople; defeat of the Byzantine Empire by the Ottoman Empire.
	ca.1455 The Gutenberg Bible is published in Germany; introduction of the movable-type printing press in the West.
1457 **Rennyo becomes the eighth head priest of the True Pure Land School.**	
	1492 Columbus arrives in the New World.
	1517 Martin Luther writes the 95 Theses, which becomes the primary catalyst for the Protestant Reformation.
	1521 The Spanish conquest of the Aztec Empire in Mexico.
	1534 Henry VIII declares himself the supreme head of the English Church.
	1543 Nicolaus Copernicus formulates heliocentric theory.
1549 Christianity arrives in Japan.	

Appendix

Japanese Text of *Tannisho*

序

ひそかに愚案を廻らしてほぼ古今を
勘うるに先師の口伝の真信に異なる
ことを歎き後学相続の疑惑あることと
を思うに、幸いに有縁の知識によらず
いかでか易行の一門に入ることを得んや
まったく自見の覚悟をもって他力の宗旨
を乱ることなかれ
よって故親鸞聖人の御物語の趣耳の底に

序

ひそかに愚案を廻らして、
ほぼ古今を勘うるに、先師
の口伝の真信に異なること
を歎き、後学相続の疑惑あ
ることを思うに、幸いに有
縁の知識によらずば、いか
でか易行の一門に入ること
を得んや。まったく自見の
覚悟をもって、他力の宗旨
を乱ることなかれ。
よって故親鸞聖人の御物

留むる所、そゞろかにこれを註す。ひとへに同心行者の不審を散ぜんがためなり

語の趣、耳の底に留むる所、いささかこれを註す。ひとへに同心行者の不審を散ぜんがためなり。

（書：くずし字）

第一章

弥陀の誓願不思議に助けられまいらせて
往生をば遂ぐるなりと信じて念仏申さん
と思いたつ心のおこるときすなわち摂取不捨
の利益にあずけしめたまうなり
弥陀の本願には老少善悪の人をえらばず
ただ信心を要とすと知るべし
そのゆえは罪悪深重煩悩熾盛の衆生を
助けんがための願にてまします

第一章

「弥陀の誓願不思議に助け
られまいらせて往生をば遂
ぐるなり」と信じて「念仏
申さん」と思いたつ心のお
こるとき、すなわち摂取不
捨の利益にあずけしめたま
うなり。

弥陀の本願には老少善悪
の人をえらばず、ただ信心
を要とすと知るべし。

そのゆえは、罪悪深重・
煩悩熾盛の衆生を助けんが
ための願にてまします。

しかれば本願を信ぜんに
は、他の善も要にあらず、
念仏にまさるべき善なきが
ゆえに、悪をもおそるべか
らず、弥陀の本願をさまた
ぐるほどの悪なきがゆえに、
と云々。

第二章

おのおのの十余ケ国の境を越えて、身命を顧みずして訪ね来らしめたまう御志、ひとえに往生極楽の道を問い聞かんがためなり。

しかるに、念仏よりほかに往生の道をも存知し、また法文等をも知りたるらんと、心にくく思し召しておわしましてはんべらば、大きなる誤りなり。

もししからば、南都北嶺にもゆゆしき学匠たち多く

座せられて候なれば、かの
人々にもあいたてまつりて、
往生の要よくよく聞かるべ
きなり。

親鸞におきては、「ただ
念仏して弥陀に助けられま
いらすべし」と、よき人の
仰せを被りて信ずるほかに、
別の子細なきなり。

念仏は、まことに浄土に
生まるるたねにてやはんべ
るらん、また地獄に堕つる
業にてやはんべるらん、総
じてもって存知せざるなり。

たとい法然聖人にすかされ

まいらせて、念仏して地獄に堕ちたりとも、さらに後悔すべからず候。

そのゆえは、自余の行を励みて仏になるべかりける身が、念仏を申して地獄にも堕ちて候わばこそ、「すかされたてまつりて」といふ後悔も候わめ。いずれの行も及び難き身なれば、とても地獄は一定すみかぞかし。

弥陀の本願まことにおわしまさば、釈尊の説教、虚言なるべからず。仏説まこ

弥陀の本願まことにおわしまさば釈尊の説教

虚言なるべからず仏説まことにおわしまさば

善導の御釈虚言したまうべからず善導の御釈

まことならば法然の仰せそらごとならんや法然の

仰せまことならば親鸞が申す旨またもってむなし

からべからず候か詮ずるところ愚身が信心におき

てはかくのごとしこのうえは念仏をとりて信

じたてまつらんともまたすてんとも面々の

御計らいなりと云々

とにおわしまさば、善導の

御釈、虚言したまうべから

ず。善導の御釈まこと なら

ば、法然の仰せ、そらごと

ならんや。法然の仰せま こ

とならば、親鸞が申す旨、

またもってむなしかるべか

らず候か。

詮ずるところ、愚身が信

心におきてはかくのごとし。

このうえは、念仏をとりて

信じたてまつらんとも、ま

たすてんとも、面々の御計

らいなり、と云々。

第三章

善人なおもって往生を遂ぐ、いわんや悪人をや。しかるを世の人つねにいわく、「悪人なおお往生す、いかにいわんや善人をや」。この条、一旦そのいわれあるに似たれども、本願他力の意趣に背けり。

そのゆえは、自力作善の人は、ひとえに他力をたのむ心欠けたる間、弥陀の本願にあらず。しかれども、自力の心をひるがえして、

ぐるなり

煩悩具足の我らは、いずれの行にても生死を

離るることあるべからざるを憐みたまいて

願をおこしたまう本意悪人成仏のため

なれば他力をたのみたてまつる悪人もっと

も往生の正因なり

よって善人だにこそ往生すれまして悪人は

と仰せ候いき

他力をたのみたてまつれば、真実報土の往生を遂ぐるなり。

煩悩具足の我らはいずれの行にても生死を離るることあるべからざるを憐みたまいて願をおこしたまう本意、悪人成仏のためなれば、他力をたのみたてまつる悪人、もっとも往生の正因なり。

よって善人だにこそ往生すれ、まして悪人は、と仰せ候いき。

第四章

慈悲に聖道・浄土のかわ
りめあり。

聖道の慈悲というは、も
のを憐れみ愛しみ育むなり。
しかれども、思うがごとく
助け遂ぐること、極めてあ
りがたし。

浄土の慈悲というは、念
仏して急ぎ仏になりて、大
慈大悲心をもって思うがご
とく衆生を利益するをいう
べきなり。

今生に、いかにいとおし

存知のごとく助け難ければ、この慈悲
始終なし。しかれば念仏申すのみぞ
末徹りたる大慈悲心にて候べきと云々

不便と思うとも、存知のご
とく助け難ければ、この慈
悲始終なし。しかれば念仏
申すのみぞ、末徹りたる大
慈悲心にて候べき、と云々。

第五章

親鸞（しんらん）は父母（ふも）の孝養（こうよう）のため
とて念仏（ねんぶつ）、一返（いっぺん）にても申（もう）し
たること、いまだ候（そうら）わず。

そのゆえは、一切（いっさい）の有情（うじょう）
は皆（みな）もって世々生々（せせしょうじょう）の父母（ふも）
兄弟（きょうだい）なり。いずれもいずれ
も、この順次生（じゅんじしょう）に仏（ぶつ）に成（な）り
て助（たす）け候（そうろ）うべきなり。

わが力（ちから）にて励（はげ）む善（ぜん）にても
候（そうら）わばこそ、念仏（ねんぶつ）を廻向（えこう）し
て父母（ふも）をも助（たす）け候（そうら）わめ、た
だ自力（じりき）をすてて急（いそ）ぎ浄土（じょうど）の
さとりを開（ひら）きなば、六道四（ろくどうし）

六道四生のあいだ、いずれの業苦に沈めりとも、神道方便をもってまず有縁を度すべきなり、と云〻。

生のあいだ、いずれの業苦に沈めりとも、神通方便をもってまず有縁を度すべきなり、と云〻。

第六章

専修念仏の輩の、「わが
弟子、ひとの弟子」という
相論の候らんこと、もって
のほかの子細なり。
親鸞は弟子一人ももたず
候。

そのゆえは、わが計らい
にて人に念仏を申させ候わ
ばこそ、弟子にても候わめ、
ひとえに弥陀の御もよおし
にあずかりて念仏申し候人
を、「わが弟子」と申すこ
と、極めたる荒涼のことな

り。

つくべき縁あれば伴い、
離るべき縁あれば離るる
とのあるをも、「師を背き
て人につれて念仏すれば、
往生すべからざるものなり」
なんどいうこと不可説なり。
如来より賜りたる信心を、
わがもの顔に取り返さんと
申すにや。かえすがえすも、
あるべからざることなり。
自然の理にあいかなわば、
仏恩をも知り、また師の恩
をも知るべきなり、と云々。

第七章

念仏者は無碍の一道なり。
そのいわれ如何とならば、
信心の行者には、天神・地
祇も敬伏し、魔界・外道も
障碍することなし。罪悪も
業報を感ずることあたわず、
諸善も及ぶことなきゆえに、
無碍の一道なり、と云々。

第八章

念仏は行者のために非行・非善なり。

わが計らいにて行ずるにあらざれば非行という、わが計らいにてつくる善にもあらざれば非善という。

ひとえに他力にして自力を離れたるゆえに、行者のためには非行・非善なり、と云々。

（書道本文・省略）

第九章

「念仏申し候えども、踊躍
歓喜の心おろそかに候こと、
また急ぎ浄土へ参りたき心
の候わぬは、いかにと候べ
きことにて候やらん」と申
しいれて候いしかば、

「親鸞もこの不審ありつる
に、唯円房、同じ心にてあ
りけり。よくよく案じみれ
ば、天におどり地におどる
ほどに喜ぶべきことを喜ば
ぬにて、いよいよ往生は一
定と思いたまうべきなり。

喜ぶべき心を抑えて喜ばせざるは、煩悩の所為なり。しかるに仏かねて知ろしめして、煩悩具足の凡夫と仰せられたることなれば、他力の悲願は、かくのごときの我らがためなりけりと知られて、いよいよ頼もしく覚ゆるなり。

また浄土へ急ぎ参りたき心のなくて、いささか所労のこともあれば、死なんずるやらんと心細く覚ゆること、煩悩の所為なり。久遠劫より今まで流転せ

る苦悩の旧里はすてがたく、
いまだ生まれざる安養の浄
土は恋しからず候こと、ま
ことによくよく煩悩の興盛
に候にこそ。
　名残惜しく思えども、娑
婆の縁つきて力なくして終
わるときに、かの土へは参
るべきなり。急ぎ参りたき
心なき者を、ことに憐れみ
たまうなり。
　これにつけてこそ、いよ
いよ大悲大願は頼もしく、
往生は決定と存じ候え。
　踊躍歓喜の心もあり、急

たく候わんには煩悩のなきやらんとあや

しく候いなまし と云々

ぎ浄土へも参りたく候わん
には、煩悩のなきやらんと、
あやしく候いなまし」と云々。

第十章

念仏には無義をもって義
とす、不可称・不可説・不
可思議のゆえに、と仰せ候
いき。

The following Appendix should be read from right to left and in reverse order, starting on page 001 at the end of this book and continuing backwards to the final page, which is 024.

The Japanese text of *Tannisho* is shown here in two formats: at the top, the cursive-style writing is by master calligrapher Taizan Kimura. Below that, the text is printed with *furigana* added to clarify the pronunciation of Chinese characters.